PENGUIN BOOKS

Let's Hear It for the Girls

Erica Bauermeister received her undergraduate degree from Occidental College and a Ph.D. in literature from the University of Washington. As a child, she was introduced to some of the greatest girls of literature by her mother. Later, when she went to school, she often wondered where the strong and brave female characters had gone. *Let's Hear It for the Girls* took her, this time with her two children, on a search to find those great girls and women once again.

Holly Smith is a lifelong reader who has been thrilled to immerse herself in the world of children's literature. For the past two years she has shared books with preschool children through weekly readings. For ten years she has managed an independent bookstore. For thirty years she has been an aunt to many nieces and nephews, both biological and chosen. Always she has encouraged reading, knowing how much it has added to her life.

Erica Bauermeister and Holly Smith are the authors, with Jesse Larsen, of *500 Great Books by Women: A Reader's Guide*.

For Kathleen!
Peter, Rachel
and Hunter —
Explorers all...
Happy reading!
Erica Bauermeister

Erica Bauermeister
and Holly Smith

Penguin

Let's Hear It for the Girls

*375 Great Books for
Readers 2–14*

PENGUIN BOOKS

Published by the Penguin Group

Penguin Books USA Inc., 375 Hudson Street,

New York, New York 10014, U.S.A.

Penguin Books Ltd, 27 Wrights Lane, London W8 5TZ, England

Penguin Books Australia Ltd, Ringwood, Victoria, Australia

Penguin Books Canada Ltd, 10 Alcorn Avenue,

Toronto, Ontario, Canada M4V 3B2

Penguin Books (N.Z.) Ltd, 182–190 Wairau Road, Auckland 10, New Zealand

Penguin Books Ltd, Registered Offices: Harmondsworth, Middlesex, England

First published in Penguin Books 1997

10 9 8 7 6 5 4 3 2 1

LIBRARY OF CONGRESS CATALOGING IN PUBLICATION DATA

Bauermeister, Erica.

   Let's hear ir for the girls: 375 great books for readers 2–14/
Erica Bauermeister and Holly Smith.

      p.   cm.

Includes indexes.

ISBN 0 14 02.5732 2

1. Children's literature—Bibliography. 2. Children's stories,
English—Bibliography. 3. Girls—Juvenile fiction—Bibliography.
4. Women—Juvenile fiction—Bibliography. 5. Girls—Juvenile
literature—Bibliography. 6. Women—Juvenile literature—
Bibliography.   I. Smith, Holly,——— II. Title.

Z6520.C5B38   1997

[PN1009.A1]

016.8088'99282—dc20   96–9791

Printed in the United States of America

Set in Bembo

Designed by Junie Lee

For Rylan, my test pilot, and Caitlin, my reading partner.
—E. B.

To some special young readers—Cierra Barnes, Brent Becker, and
Holly Sandborg—for full lives enriched with books.
—H. S.

PREFACE

> *The power of the imagination—the sound of the heart. What can we do? I think one thing we can do is share with children works of the imagination—those sounds deepest in the human heart, often couched in symbol and metaphor. These don't give children packaged answers. They invite children to go within themselves to listen to the sounds of their own hearts.*
>
> Katherine Paterson, writer

Remember snuggling your small body next to a grown-up, listening to the pages rustle, the intense exhilaration of the first time you cracked the code and realized that $c + a + t$ equaled a word you knew. Remember the smell of a musty old library on a hot summer afternoon or the joy of a stolen hour under the covers, pages illuminated by flashlight. If, in the bustle of your grown-up life, you have forgotten, ask a child. Children know; they can tell you. Books are magic. Reading is power. Open a book and you enter a world far beyond your own.

What an extraordinary world it is, filled with characters to be lost in and rhythms to shape the music of your thoughts. Books are a room of one's own, a blast of fresh air, a friend who will never, ever desert you. They show you the best, and worst, of yourself. They introduce you to dancers, doctors, writers, archaeologists, politicians, sled dog racers, dreamers—and suddenly you realize that's what you want to be, that's what you already are, inside.

It is impossible to overestimate the power books have over us. Ask your friends what books they recall from their childhood; ask children their favorites. Watch their eyes, listen to their excitement. These are books that reached deep into our souls and shaped us—what we want from life, what we care about, who we become. Having access to books that bring out the best in us is crucial to our development. This is particularly true for girls, who often have to battle messages that tell them they are second best, or victims, or human beings measured by the beauty of their bodies and the pliability of their minds.

We have created this guide with a belief in the power of books to give children a vision of what is possible. *Let's Hear It for the Girls* provides one way for adults and young readers to find fiction and nonfiction books featuring female protagonists of all colors, classes, and nationalities. We've included longtime favorites—*The Little House in the Big Woods*, *Island of the Blue Dolphins*, *A Wrinkle in Time*—as well as many new discoveries including books about little Anne Marie of Barbados, fossil-hunter Mary Anning from the nineteenth century, Shabanu of the Cholistan desert, and Savitri from an Indian folk tale more than two thousand years old. Through these books, we travel through time, around and beyond our planet.

In making our selections, we looked for books with strong and resourceful girls and women. These fictional characters and real people could be doing extravagant things—outwitting a dragon, winning a Nobel Prize, or surviving alone in the wilderness. But there is much that is extraordinary in everyday lives: Anna teaches her grandmother to read, Linnea travels to Monet's garden, Kyla lets her little sister copy her every move, Izumi loves caterpillars even when no one around her understands. These girls and women teach us that "greatness" can be defined in many ways.

But characters weren't our only criterion for selection. A picture book is also visual art; the written word is also music. Books that broadcast their messages with a bullhorn, or whose words fall off the page like boulders onto a highway, are no fun to read. We wanted to find books that inspire on many levels and explore the beauty of language and art. We looked for books that pull you in, that make readers forget they've been called for dinner. We wanted books that young readers, when they grow up, will remember and read to the children in their lives.

There were other, more practical considerations as well. So that all the books would be available, we made sure that each book was in print as of February 1996. In order to encourage diversity among writers, we included no more than one illustrated and one chapter book per author. We recognize that many authors have written numerous books worth reading, and it is our hope you will use these selections as a springboard for your own explorations. For those of you who may find a favorite book missing from the "Moving On" section—*Little Women*, or Anne Frank's diary, for example—we encourage you to look through our guide *500 Great Books by Women* for these and other suggestions.

The books we chose for *Let's Hear It for the Girls* have been arranged alphabetically by title in four different sections which allow for the different reading and comprehension levels among children: "Picture Books" (approximate ages 2–5), "Storybooks" (3–8), "Chapter Books" (6–11), and "Moving On" (10 and older). Because reading and comprehension skills vary so dramatically from child to child, and because children often appreciate hearing more difficult books aloud, or at times want the comfort of an old favorite, we encourage you to browse across all levels. In order to help you find particular books or follow special interests, we have included cross-reference indexes by author, title, time period of the book, genre, country of book content, and subject.

So here they are, books and girls bursting with exuberance, glowing with life, complicated in their confusions, intent upon their discoveries. Girls and women meeting once-in-a-lifetime challenges or dealing with daily routine; books that make you laugh or cry and give you a vision of another life. May they help make you and the children in your life strong and brave and full of dreams.

ACKNOWLEDGMENTS

This book would not exist without the persistent encouragement of our agent, Elizabeth Frost Knappman, New England Publishing Associates, Inc., and the enthusiasm of Caroline White, our editor. The research for this book was wide-reaching, and there are many more who deserve thanks than can be listed here. Jon Takemoto and Kim Larson, librarians at the Wallingford-Wilmot Library in Seattle, were always resourceful and ever patient. Ben Bauermeister served as both personal computer guru and entertaining storyteller. Jody Fickes Shapiro, Marilyn Hanna-Myrick, Joyce Denebrink, Donna Nichols-White, Mary Jo Bauermeister, Bill Meierding, Whitney Ricketts, Suzanne Shaw, Mici Walker, Janus Adams, Myra and David Sadker, and Lucy Buckley were sources of marvelous advice and book titles. The elementary students at Pacific Crest Schools and the preschool children at Denise Louie Education Center in Seattle opened their ears, eyes, and minds and told us what they thought about books. People from all around the country responded to our request, and wrote us their memories and feelings about reading. Special thanks are also due to Second Story Books, Elliott Bay Book Company, and the many other bookstores that generously allowed us to roam their shelves and databases, hour after hour. The National Women's History Project was an invaluable resource and a source of many suggestions. To all the publishers who greeted our project so enthusiastically and supplied us with books to review, a smile of gratitude and a bow of respect for your work. And, of course, the deepest of appreciation for the authors of the thousands of books we read, for their dedication to the impact, importance, and delight of the written word.

You can't write books and raise children at the same time without a tremendous amount of help. So first, a profound thank-you to my husband, Ben, who makes my work possible and my life full of joy. My children, Caitlin and Rylan, greeted every box of books with excitement, and all the deadlines with admirable patience. Dorothy Rechtin proved that mothers can edit their children's work. My writing group, Lynne Auld and Susan Fleagle, made sense out of half-baked ideas. And always there's Holly Smith, the best of friends and work partners. Thank you. —E. B.

Deepest gratitude goes to my friend Erica Bauermeister for support and encouragement above and beyond the role of co-writer. Many thanks to my mom, Sally, my weekly dinner partner, who listened intently as the book progressed. Gerry and Cubby Smith and Jan and Rick Cook generously gave me places to stay that allowed for concentration and creativity difficult to get at home. Kudos to Annie Links, Kim Ricketts, Ian Sowers—fellow booksellers and word lovers. And again, thanks to my family and friends, whose support, in ways too numerous to mention, helps define me and my writing. —H. S.

Contents

Let's Hear It for the Girls

PICTURE BOOKS
AGES 2–5

> *In these books the vocabulary is simple, with text of a few sentences per page. Illustrations range from bold and abstract to realistic and highly detailed. It's a pleasure to take the time to become absorbed in these other worlds with your child.*

As a child not yet ready to read, you anticipate the times when one of those big, busy people picks you up and puts you in their lap. Your curves and angles blend together and life slows down and centers. Whatever happened before—the whirlwind of your day, the frustration of not being big enough—all disappears as the book opens.

Your eyes are drawn to the colors first. Sometimes they're bright, loud ones that go straight to your stomach and tickle. Other times they are soft and gentle, like a blanket tucked around you. Your grown-up knows the words that surround the pictures, and as the voice goes up and down, floating around you, the words gather meaning to become stories. The stories can be quiet, or silly, or make you want to run and jump and explore the world. Each one is different. And here in the warm circle of someone's arms, you learn that you love stories.

Abuela, Arthur Dorros, illustrated by Elisa Kleven, *1991, United States,* FANTASY

Abuela and her granddaughter are always ready for an adventure. While feeding birds in Central Park, they wonder what it would be like to fly. So off they go, soaring on the wings of imagination high above New York City. Past the Statue of Liberty they fly; *"Me gusta,"* Abuela says, for the Statue of Liberty reminds her of when she first came to this country. They sail through the clouds, naming all their shapes in English and Spanish, resting for a minute in a cloud chair. When they pass Papa's window at work, Abuela does a flip just for the fun of it. The busy and appealing illustrations capture both the intensity of city life and the joy between a girl and her grandmother. Landing safely back in the park, the granddaughter sees Abuela eyeing the boat rides—perhaps another excursion?

> *The greatest fun in reading aloud lies in the adventure of the thing—the sense of taking a child on an exploration of a fascinating territory into which you alone have penetrated.*
>
> *Leonard Wibberley, writer*

Amelia's Fantastic Flight, Rose Bursik, author and illustrator, *1992, United States,* FANTASY

"Amelia liked airplanes. So she built one." Bright red and just the right size for one small person, it's perfect for intrepid Amelia, who now proceeds on "a little spin" around the world. "She breezed through Brazil, and got a kick out of Kenya." Each country is granted its own page, with intricate illustrations of the flora, fauna, or architecture that characterizes it. At the top of each page is a map of the world, with the route Amelia took to get from one destination to the next. Even little children will love tracing travel routes, sounding out country names, and finding objects and animals in the pictures. Through each picture goes Amelia in her jaunty little plane, teaching geography in a delightful way.

Angela's Wings, Eric Jon Nones, author and illustrator, *1995, United States,* FANTASY

It just happens one morning; when Angela wakes up, she has wings. "Oh, terrific," she says, "what am I supposed to do with these?" Hoping no one will notice, she goes into the kitchen, but these big, beautiful wings are pretty hard to miss. On the street, at school, everybody comments about them and it makes Angela uncomfortable. But Grandma's words of wisdom set Angela free: "Everyone's got something special, child. Just depends on what you do with it, that's all." Now you should see her on the basketball court or at the Christmas play or keeping company with kites. Eric Jon Nones's realistic illustrations, with their expressive faces full of emotions, add to the humor of Angela's dilemma and the joy of her resolution.

Annie Bananie, Leah Komaiko, illustrated by Laura Cornell, *1987, United States,* POETRY

Annie Bananie is the best kind of friend, who "promised we would always play, now Annie Bananie's going away." So her girlfriend, the narrator of this story, reminds Annie Bananie of all the fun they've had. The friendship of these five-year-olds includes memories of writing with cockroach blood and tickling bumblebees, riding ferris wheels and taking baths together, to name a few. Leah Komaiko's exuberant *Annie Bananie* combines a rhyming text with wild, vivid illustrations sure to entertain both the child and the reader.

Bamboozled, David Legge, author and illustrator, *1995, United States,* FANTASY

Get ready for a feast for the eyes and a tickle for the funny bone with this story. A young granddaughter visits her beloved Grandpa every week, but this week things feel different. The realistic watercolors could be glanced at quickly, but then something catches your eye—over there in the corner, why is that goose in green galoshes and a yellow rain hat? Is the bottom of that floor lamp really a flowerpot? On each page, as she and Grandpa do the things they do—play cards, drink tea, work in the yard—the little girl just can't seem to put her finger on what feels different. Children love looking at the fantastic artwork and searching for the unusual; the more they look, the more they see. Finally the little girl figures out what is so odd: Grandpa's socks don't match! They have a good laugh together (with the elephant, goose, monkey, and penguin) and she gets in her paddleboat and waves her good-bye.

> *I'll always remember just Mama and me and the night that we walked by the big big sea.*
> *from* The Big Big Sea *by Martin Waddell*

The Big Big Sea, Martin Waddell, illustrated by Jennifer Eachus, *1994, Ireland,* FICTION

There are moments with our parents we remember throughout our lives—*The Big Big Sea* describes one of these. A little girl and her mother take a night walk on the beach. In simple prose, the book describes how they run and splash in the water, sit quietly on the sand, and finally come home for hot buttered toast. The illustrations capture the night and the serenity of the setting with dark colors relieved by bits of muted blues, yellows, and pinks. At one point, Mama says, "Remember this time. It's the way life should be." For adults and children, it's a book to remind you to make—and treasure—times like these.

Can't Sit Still, Karen E. Lotz, illustrated by Colleen Browning, *1993, United States,* FICTION

Can't Sit Still is a quick blast of sunshine, a book that will appeal to all those kids with extra energy. The illustrations reverberate off the pages in bright yellows, blues, oranges, and greens as a young inner-city girl hops, jumps, skips, and rides her way through the seasons of one year. The words are as quick as the girl herself: "pump the pedals / race the sun / slipping / sliding / down the block /

wind smells like hot java beans / tickles the hairs on the back of my neck." For those who like wordplay and rhythms, *Can't Sit Still* can't be beat.

Come away from the water, Shirley, John Burningham, author and illustrator, *1977, United States,* FANTASY

Shirley and her parents spend a day at the seashore. Shirley's parents read, knit, and concern themselves with mundane issues like smelly seaweed and tar on the beach. Juxtaposing the pages featuring Shirley's boring parents are colorful, wordless illustrations of Shirley and her wild seaside adventures. There's a pirate ship, a sword fight, and an island with a buried treasure—and poor Shirley's parents don't even know. A humorous book about an inventive kid and parents who just don't get it, *Come away from the water, Shirley* lets young children and their grown-ups laugh their way across the generation gap.

> *Some things can only be said in fiction, but that doesn't mean they aren't true.*
>
> *Aaron Latham, writer*

Dial-a-Croc, Mike Dumbleton, illustrated by Ann James, *1991, Australia,* FICTION

Vanessa wants to make some money, so she takes herself "out in the outback, beyond the Back of Beyond" and captures a crocodile. She sells his skills and soon he is the star attraction at a house of horrors, punching tickets at a railroad station, or rescuing people in accidents, while Vanessa gets rich. But Vanessa notices that the richer she becomes, the sadder her crocodile looks. He longs for his home and friends, and tells Vanessa she can be his breakfast or take him back home. She chooses wisely and although she will miss him, she hugs her croc when they part. Mischievous Vanessa is gleefully portrayed as she rides her crocodile, talks on her car phone, or receives an unexpected gift at the story's end.

Do Like Kyla, Angela Johnson, illustrated by James Ransome, *1990,*
United States, FICTION

Everything Kyla does, her little sister does, too—and the beauty
of this book is that this is just fine with both of them. When Kyla
puts on a sweater, so does her sister; if Kyla has purple snow boots,
her sister does, too. Going to the store, little sister steps in big sister's
footprints. But the beauty, and the little surprise, of the book is that
at the end of the day, it is little sister who taps the window good
night first, and "Kyla does just like me." Tired of hearing about sibling rivalry? Here is a story that offers a warm and loving contrast.

Grandmother and I, Helen E. Buckley, illustrated by Jan Ormerod,
1994, United States, FICTION

Everybody's lap is good for something—Mom's is good for
when you need your hair braided or your shoes tied; Dad's is good
for playing cowboy. Siblings will read to you, but then you have to sit
beside them, so their laps don't count. Grandmother's lap, though, is
special, the place you want to be when you have a bad cold, or there
is lightning outside, or your cat has been missing for days: "We sit in
the big chair and rock back and forth, back and forth. And Grandmother hums little tunes. And her shoes make a soft sound on the
floor." *Grandmother and I* is the kind of book that's perfect for soothing a little one—at bedtime, skinned-knee time, or after a rough day
at preschool.

> *Books are dreams you can hold in your hand. Dreams are books*
> *without pages.*
>
> *Sundaira Morninghouse, writer*

Hairs = Pelitos, Sandra Cisneros, illustrated by Terry Ybanez, *1984,*
United States, FICTION

Most people have hair on their head, and the little girl in this
story tells us all about the hairs in her family. The narrator has hair
that is lazy, her Papa's is like a broom, a sister has hair that is slippery,

a brother's is like fur. But it is Mama's hair that brings this young girl comfort, warmth, and joy. Simple, bold illustrations give visual stimulation for young children as they show hair that is orange or black or brown, on people who are purple, pink, or green. The text, in Spanish and English, offers the reader a chance to read in two languages.

Harriet and the Promised Land, Jacob Lawrence, author and illustrator, *1968, United States,* BIOGRAPHY

Jacob Lawrence is a well-known and critically acclaimed artist who draws on his African American heritage to create paintings of high contrast and emotional intensity, in which dark skin stands in sharp and proud relief against bright and vivid reds, blues, whites, and yellows. In *Harriet and the Promised Land*, he has written a poem simple enough for young children to understand that deals honestly with the harsh reality of slavery and glorifies both Harriet Tubman's physical strength and her unwavering resolve to help other slaves escape to the North. This striking book gives children an introduction to both a gifted painter and a courageous woman.

Hazel's Amazing Mother, Rosemary Wells, author and illustrator, *1985, United States,* FANTASY

Hazel takes a trip by herself into town to buy things for a picnic lunch with her mother, but on the way home she gets lost and then is confronted by a gang of kids who take her doll away. Now things get exciting. Across town, Hazel's mother is carried off by a great wind and lands in the tree right above Hazel and her tormentors. Her disembodied voice orders the bullies about until all is set to rights again. Grown-ups may find the story improbable, but there is something distinctly reassuring to children in the Avenging Mother, and it's hard not to giggle at the expressions on the bullies' faces when the tables are turned.

I Like Me!, Nancy Carlson, author and illustrator, *1988, United States,* FICTION

The happy, happy pig in *I Like Me!* exudes self-confidence. She is her own best friend, a pig who can ride her bike (with training wheels) very fast; who likes her tail, tummy, and toes; and who, when she makes a mistake, tries and tries again. The bold, enthusiastic illustrations capture this assured little pig and are a delight to children's eyes. This book shouts to be read aloud; its bolstering feelings are infectious.

> Reading . . . seems to set the course for the day ahead, to bring closure at night.
>
> Terri de la Peña, writer

Imogene's Antlers, David Small, author and illustrator, *1985, United States,* FANTASY

"On Thursday, when Imogene woke up, she found she had grown antlers." Big ones, in fact. They soar above her head like the wings of a great airplane as she sits in bed, a bit bemused. Imogene's brother Norman declares she has turned into a rare form of miniature elk; Imogene's mother spends the day in fainting fits. Imogene just carries on throughout her day. Lucy, the kitchen maid, uses the antlers to hang dish towels; the cook slips doughnuts on them and sends Imogene out to feed the birds. It's all a great deal of fun, and the next morning, the antlers are gone. But the story's not over yet . . .

Is That Josie?, Keiko Narahashi, author and illustrator, *1994, United States,* FICTION

Josie is an imaginative little girl who spends her day pretending to be everything but Josie. That's not Josie peeking out of her bed, it's a sly fox; it's not Josie who's building that tower but an ant in an anthill; and that little girl eating the blueberry pie? Well, that's a hippopotamus. What's fun about this book is the creativity of Josie's imagination and her joyful approach to life. The simple, repetitive text, the beguiling watercolor-and-ink illustrations, and the ever-popular theme of hiding and disguising make this a great early book choice.

Knoxville, Tennessee, Nikki Giovanni, illustrated by Larry Johnson, *1968, United States,* POETRY

Knoxville, Tennessee is a poem of few words, spread out over pages heavy with the vibrating greens of grass and trees, the bright whites of summer dresses, the deep skin colors of a little girl's family and friends, the cloudless blue of the sky, the brilliant yellow of an ear of corn. The poem tells of digging in daddy's garden, going to church picnics, running barefoot, being with grandparents. Few books so completely capture the lushness of summers in the Southeastern United States, or the warmth of family relationships.

> *A child's story reading if it is rich lays open a world that lasts a lifetime; an impoverished, banal story world dulls the spirit forever.*
>
> *Angus Wilson, writer*

A Letter to the King, Leong Vá, author and illustrator, *1987, China,* FOLKLORE

More than two thousand years ago, a Chinese king wrote down this story. It is unknown whether it is fact or fiction, but Leong Vá has written a delicious retelling, accompanied by pen-and-ink illustrations that use spare but arresting detail to create a feeling of motion. When a relative of the king dies in a small village, the king sentences the village doctor to prison. The doctor, who has five daughters and no sons, laments that a son would help him, not weep like his daughters. Ti Ying, his youngest, foresees the pain and suffering that will happen if her village has no doctor, so she goes to the Forbidden City and writes the king a letter defending her father. No one will deliver it—she's just a girl and is ignored by priests and guards. Ti Ying is clever, though, and finds a way to deliver her letter, which both impresses the king and saves her father.

The Little Brown Jay: A Tale from India, Elizabeth Claire, illustrated by Miriam Katin, *1992, India,* FOLKLORE

A beautiful princess with a harsh voice, a plain brown jay with an exquisite song, and a magic lotus flower make *The Little Brown Jay* a wonderful introduction to folklore for young children. This book is filled with enchanting, colorful illustrations, and there is a happy ending for the princess and a blind prince. But the happiest of all is the jaybird. With a little belief in magic, even the youngest of children will enjoy this kind tale of generosity.

The Little Engine That Could, Watty Piper, illustrated by George and Doris Hauman, *1930, United States,* FICTION

Generations of children have thrilled to the courage and steadfastness of the little blue engine, who helps a stranded train after the shiny new engine, the big strong engine, and the old tired engine have all refused. Even though she has only been used for switching engines in the yard, and isn't sure she has the strength for the job, the little blue engine takes pity on the train filled with toys and good food destined for the children on the other side of the mountain. Repeating her mantra of "I think I can I think I can I think I can," she chugs her way to victory. A grinning clown, stuffed elephants, bears, tin soldiers, and picture-perfect dolls cheer her on. A story as wholesome and satisfying as warm oatmeal on a cold morning, it teaches the value of sympathy, selflessness, and self-confidence.

Madeline, Ludwig Bemelmans, author and illustrator, *1939, France,* POETRY

Paris, poetry, and Madeline have held children's attention now for nearly sixty years in Ludwig Bemelmans's *Madeline*. Madeline is the smallest of the girls at the convent school, but she is also the bravest and a bit of a class clown. When she is whisked off to the hospital in the middle of the night, all of her classmates are worried. But when they visit her, besides the toys and dolls in her hospital room, she now has a scar from her appendix operation! It figures, Madeline would be the lucky one to get a scar, and before long, all the girls want to have their appendixes out, too. Ludwig Bemelmans's busy drawings of famous Parisian architecture and his rhythmic verse are delightful. You may want to follow Madeline in the five sequels to this book.

> *My favorite book was* Madeline . . . *I loved that book! . . . I thought the [library] copy I had hidden was the only copy in the whole world. I knew it was wrong to hide the book, but there was no way I was going to part with* Madeline. *I memorized the words in the book, and though I couldn't really read, I pretended that I could.*
>
> Judy Blume, *writer*

Mama Went Walking, Christine Berry, illustrated by Maria Cristina Brusca, *1990, United States,* FANTASY

Sarah's mom likes to go on adventures and when Mama goes adventuring, Sarah is never far behind. The rhythmic text describing these explorations makes this book fun to read aloud, and the imaginative watercolors humorously play off the story. We go with Mama into the Jaba-Jaba Jungle, canoe with her down the Rattlesnake River, or ride with her in Ropacactus Canyon. With each adventure, Sarah comes to Mama's rescue. It's when Sarah follows Mama into the Gonagetcha Forest, though, that Mama ends up rescuing Sarah, bringing their love and support for each other full circle.

The Mommy Exchange, Amy Hest, illustrated by DyAnne DiSalvo-Ryan, *1988, United States,* FICTION

Jessica is sure that her friend Jason has a much better life. He gets spaghetti more often, his mom keeps his room clean, and the laundry is always done so he never has to wear mismatched pajamas. Jason likes the excitement at Jessica's house—with the twin babies, there is always something going on, and besides, neat is boring. Jessica decides they need to exchange mommies, for keeps; the mommies decide to try it for a weekend. It lasts one night. *The Mommy Exchange* is a child-size version of the grass-is-always-greener syndrome—because in the end, nobody tucks you into bed like Mommy.

My Father's Hands, Joanne Ryder, illustrated by Mark Graham, *1994, United States,* FICTION

"No one will ever bring me better treasures than the ones cupped in my father's hands," says a young girl after a day spent in the garden with her father. There have been pink worms, a snail that slides over her father's dirt-covered hands, and a bug-eyed praying mantis. For father and daughter, each discovery is a marvel. Mark Graham's paintings illuminate the young girl's sense of awe and curiosity as she watches each animal, completely absorbed and delighted. This wonderful book celebrates the love and trust between a daughter and father, and their shared reverence for nature.

No Peas for Nellie, Chris L. Demarest, author and illustrator, *1988, United States,* FICTION

Nellie is an imaginative picky eater. No thanks to peas, she doesn't like them; Nellie would rather eat an aardvark, a spider, a slimy salamander, maybe even a big old crocodile. In her imagination, and through a series of hilarious cartoon illustrations, Nellie pursues her exotic taste treats. You've got to smile at the aghast expression on the face of a hairy warthog as Nellie crawls toward him, dinner knife in mouth; or the befuddlement of a python, as Nellie drags him by his tail toward a waiting and ready hot dog bun. And look closely, for all the while, a series of ants are marching across the pages with Nellie's peas. At the story's end, the peas are gone, but there is still the milk . . .

The Paper Bag Princess, Robert N. Munsch, illustrated by Michael Martchenko, *1980, Canada,* FANTASY

Robert Munsch writes with the exuberance of a five-year-old after three chocolate bars. He always bends the rules of society just a bit, just enough to make it fun. *The Paper Bag Princess* has become a classic, and spawned many imitations. But nothing can beat Elizabeth, left in the ashes of her castle with nothing to wear, while the dragon carries off her beloved Prince Ronald. Well, that makes Elizabeth angry, so after creating a frock from a paper bag (all that's left), she sets off to save Ronald, which she does by outwitting the dragon. But what's this? Ronald is not thrilled by her messy hair and outfit *de papier*. We'll leave the conclusion for you to chuckle over yourself.

> *For children, the joy of a book is not merely the story but the feel, the taste, the smell of it—the texture of the paper, the size and shape of the typeface, the illustrations, flaws, marks, even the numbering of the pages.*
>
> *Pamela Brown, writer*

Play with Me, Marie Hall Ets, author and illustrator, *1955, United States,* FICTION

Through a meadow lit by a bright and shining sun walks a sturdy little blond-haired girl in a white pinafore. Every animal she sees—a grasshopper, frog, bird, snake, fawn, turtle—fills her with big-eyed wonder. She asks each one, "Will you play with me?" and each one scurries, flies, runs, slips away. Finally, she sits sadly by the pond, and because she is quiet, one by one the animals come back until "all of them—ALL OF THEM—were playing with me." Beige background and pencil-sketch outlines provide a backdrop for the bits of color that come from the girl's hair and the animals. On each page, a bright white sun smiles down as it watches one little girl learn about nature.

Rain Talk, Mary Serfozo, illustrated by Keiko Narahashi, *1990, United States,* FICTION

A little watercolor girl plays in the rain, listening to all the sounds it makes—the "Ploomp, Ploomp, Ploomp" in the dust, the "PlipPlipPlipPlip" on the pond's surface, the "Ping Ping Pingading" on the tin shed roof. Finally, reluctantly, she has to go inside. But even then, she can still hear the various sounds the rain can make. She opens her ears and herself up joyously to each experience, becoming a part of it. Even her dress—watercolor on the run—makes her a part of her environment.

> *I believe children, even the youngest, love good language, and that they see, feel, understand and communicate more not less, than grownups.*
>
> Lucy M. Boston, *writer*

Rose Meets Mr. Wintergarten, Bob Graham, author and illustrator, *1992, England,* FICTION

The Summerses have a bright and shiny little house, and the first day they moved in they planted flowers. Mr. Wintergarten's mansion next door is gray and imposing, with huge, fantastic cactuslike plants. Even the sun won't touch Mr. Wintergarten's house, and if your ball goes over his fence, forget it. Rumor has it that he eats children and owns a crocodile. But Rose Summers's ball lands in his yard, and armed with flowers and her mother's cookies, Rose goes to get it back. The pictures are infectious, and even grown-ups, who can probably see the end coming a mile away, will delight in Rose's victory.

Sally and the Limpet, Simon James, author and illustrator, *1990, England,* FICTION

It all begins innocently enough. Sally is playing in a tide pool at the beach and what should she find but a big, bright limpet shell that she wants to take home. She tugs so hard she falls into the water and when she gets up, the limpet is on her finger. Now it won't come off, not even when her dad uses his tools, or her brother offers it food; finally Sally ends up at the doctor's office. All this fuss is too much for Sally, so she kicks over the doctor's chair and runs to the beach. She has her own simple plan for getting the limpet off. The whimsical illustrations wonderfully capture Sally's curiosity, determination, and, ultimately, satisfaction.

Silent Lotus, Jeanne M. Lee, author and illustrator, *1991, Cambodia,* FICTION

When their daughter is born, her parents name her Lotus after the blossoms on the lake. As she grows and they realize that she cannot hear and won't ever speak, they make a flower with their fingers and in that way, Lotus learns her name. They love Lotus, and they watch with delight when they see her mimicking the graceful movements of the egrets and cranes at the lake's edge, yet they see a sadness and loneliness in her eyes. Constantly they look for an omen from the gods for a path to her happiness. It is on a visit to the temple, as Lotus imitates the temple dancers, that her parents find the long-awaited sign. For there Lotus learns to "speak with her hands, body, and feet." With watercolors that are rich in color and bold in design, Jeanne Lee brings twelfth-century Cambodia and Lotus's joy to life.

> *Reader Teacher, Reader Teacher. Read me a story. Read me a story!*
>
> *Kaila Yoshitomi, preschooler*

The Trek, Ann Jonas, author and illustrator, *1985, United States,* FICTION

In *The Trek*, readers accompany a young girl on her way to school. This girl has a powerful imagination: she makes jungles out of fruit stands, deserts out of trees and grasses, and mountains out of stairways. She uses "her amazing skills that save [her] day after day," as she makes her way to the safety of school. Children will have fun trying to find all the animals hidden in the vivid illustrations. Luckily, there's a key in the back of the book showing the animals and giving their proper names.

Tucking Mommy In, Morag Loh, illustrated by Donna Rawlins, *1987, Australia,* FICTION

One night Mommy is so tired that she "can't think straight." Sue, her older daughter, offers to tell a bedtime story so Mommy won't have to think at all. Younger daughter Jenny has her doubts about this, and hopes for a good story. Wouldn't you know it, Mommy falls asleep during Sue's story, and she still has her clothes on. Jenny and Sue shake and shout and finally wake Mommy up and tell her she had better get to bed. With their help, Mommy gets into her pajamas, is tucked in, and soon falls fast asleep. Sue and Jenny tell Daddy all about it when he comes home from work, and then he tucks them in. The homey, subdued illustrations add much to the pleasure of this book.

> *We believe in books. Somehow we want to make childhood better, and we believe that a book given at the right moment can work magic in a child's life.*
>
> *Ann Schlee, writer*

Umbrella, Taro Yashima, author and illustrator, *1958, United States,* FICTION

For her third birthday, Momo gets an umbrella and red rubber boots. Then she waits for rain. Every day, waiting, she tells her mother reasons why she needs to use her umbrella—the sun is shining too brightly, or the wind might bother her eyes. But her mother tells her to keep it for a rainy day. When that day finally arrives, Momo proudly dons her boots and holds her umbrella all by herself. Without her realizing it, the umbrella has moved Momo a little further down the road of independence.

The Very Busy Spider, Eric Carle, author and illustrator, *1984, United States,* FICTION

Young children understand busyness; they can become absorbed in figuring out how to unlock the belts on their highchairs, or in creating a tower as tall as themselves. So the very busy spider, so intent upon building her web that she ignores all the other farm animals, is a kindred spirit to many. Through repetitive text the animals present the spider with many options—eating grass, chasing cats, rolling in the mud—but she keeps on, and her web grows. In the end, she is victorious—she catches a fly—and deservedly tired. Eric Carle's books for young children tend to be interactive; in this case, children get to see, and feel, the spider's bumpy body and follow the process as the raised texture of the web grows from a few shiny strands to a delicate and complicated piece of art.

When I'm Sleepy, Jane R. Howard, illustrated by Lynne Cherry, *1985, United States,* FICTION

Lying in her bed, the young narrator imagines all the places and ways she could sleep—in a nest, in a cat basket, hanging upside down like a bat, standing up like a giraffe, perched on a tree branch like an owl. While some of the situations might sound uncomfortable, they aren't, because in every case she is protected and cuddled by an animal appropriate to the setting. Goats provide a soft bed on a rocky mountain ledge, raccoon arms encircle her in a hollow log, bears provide warmth in a winter cave. In every picture the child is serenely, completely, safely asleep. *When I'm Sleepy* almost guarantees to close your little one's eyes at the end of the day and leave everyone feeling relaxed.

> *Repeat reading for me shares a few things with hot-water bottles and thumb-sucking; comfort, familiarity, the recurrence of the expected.*
>
> *Margaret Atwood, writer*

Where Are You Going, Manyoni?, Catherine Stock, author and illustrator, *1993, Zimbabwe,* FICTION

Young Manyoni rises early and slips on her blue dress. After a bowl of hot porridge, she sets off across the countryside of her native

Zimbabwe, passing huge baobab trees, malala palms, baboons, impalas, zebras—all depicted in graceful, detailed watercolors. As the illustrations take on a larger perspective, Manyoni becomes a small part of a spacious landscape. Yet while the parameters of Manyoni's environment are immense, Manyoni has nothing to fear, and the reader becomes immersed in the beauty of the wilderness through which she walks. When Manyoni meets her friend, they hurry on. And where are they going, after such a long way? To school. An excellent beginning point for discussions of different cultures, Catherine Stock's book is also a glorious introduction to rural Zimbabwe.

Wild Wild Sunflower Child Anna, Nancy White Carlstrom, illustrated by Jerry Pinkney, *1987, United States,* POETRY

Under Nancy White Carlstrom's direction, words roll and romp like puppies in the sunshine, and her characters share that sense of joy and playfulness. Little Anna rushes headlong into her exploration with nature, picking berries, rolling down grassy hills, hopping from stone to stone across a stream, dreaming in meadows, and climbing trees. Jerry Pinkney's watercolor illustrations bring us brown-skinned Anna in her bright yellow dress while the words leap and giggle across the page: "Flying in the field / in the greening / of the morning. / Anna drifts, / Anna glides, / Anna's arms open wide / for the sun rolling / sky falling. / It doesn't, Anna does. / Dizzy, tizzy Anna."

Books become friends.

Kyle Lanza, software engineer

STORYBOOKS
AGES 3–8

These books feature more elaborate texts—a paragraph to a full page of text—with illustrations that enhance the story. Reading and talking about these books with children gain you a view into their understanding of the world.

Now that no one would dare call you a baby, you're beginning to find that those first books aren't as exciting anymore. They can be fun, like going back to a place you know well. But it's more exciting now if you don't know where the story is going to go, or what will happen to the characters. Why is grandmother's lotus seed so very important? How will the bakerwoman outsmart the fairies?

Sometimes it feels as if both your body and mind are hungry. Maybe you used to chew on books because they felt good against your teething gums. Now books feed your mind, and there are days when no adult will read long enough to satisfy you. But that's all right, because in the meantime there are pictures, glorious and complicated, full of their own jokes and stories. You pick a book and start on your own journey, with no seat belts or restraining hands.

> *When you read to a child, when you put a book in a child's hands, you are bringing that child news of the infinitely varied nature of life. You are an awakener.*
>
> *Paula Fox, writer*

Amazing Grace, Mary Hoffman, illustrated by Caroline Binch, *1991, United States,* FICTION

Grace loves stories. She loves hearing them and acting them out. Some days she's Joan of Arc, or Anansi the Spider, or a peg-leg pirate. When her teacher announces that the class is going to do *Peter Pan*, Grace decides she wants to play Peter. Raj tells her she can't, because she is a girl. Natalie whispers Grace can't, because she is black. But Grace's mother and grandmother tell her she can be anything she wants to be—and Grace is a fantastic Peter Pan. The story is inspiring, but what makes this book soar are the illustrations. Caroline Binch brings Grace alive; you can feel her imagination, enthusiasm, strength, and confidence pulsing off the pages.

Angel Child, Dragon Child, Michele Maria Surat, illustrated by Vo-Dind Mai, *1983, United States,* FICTION

Ut and her family have recently moved to the United States from Vietnam, leaving behind Ut's mother because there was not enough money to bring everyone. Every day Ut misses her mother. When school begins, Raymond, the "boy with fire-colored hair," teases Ut and her sisters. Ut tries to be good—an angel child—as her mother would want, but sometimes she is a dragon child and fights back. As punishment for one of these fights, she is forced to spend time with Raymond. Alone in the classroom, they get to know each other, and eventually it is Raymond who comes up with the idea that helps reunite Ut and her mother. The expressive illustrations show Ut's loneliness, frustrations, happiness with her new friend, and wholehearted joy when her mother arrives. An excellent choice for a wide range of readers, *Angel Child, Dragon Child* also includes helpful pronunciations of Vietnamese words.

Annabelle Swift, Kindergartner, Amy Schwartz, author and illustrator, *1988, United States,* FICTION

Annabelle's sister Lucy—she's in third grade—wants to teach Annabelle a few things she'll need to know for kindergarten. Annabelle's a good learner, but the lessons don't feel very helpful once she's at school. The kindergarten teacher doesn't talk about geography, and although Lucy says colors have names like Raving Scarlet and Blue Desire, everyone else just calls them red and blue. This humorous book will be enjoyed by kids who are changing schools or day-care centers and are afraid of making mistakes. Thankfully, one of the lessons Annabelle learns from her sister wins her the praise of her teacher and classmates and bolsters her confidence.

> *I regularly dragged home the whole ten [books from the library], and it wasn't easy. They came in such a variety of shapes and sizes—square, tall, thin, fattish, large, small—and they always slipped and slid against each other. But this was part of their charm. The books my mother and father read all seemed to be exactly the same size and shape. I think I believed they all said exactly the same thing inside.*
>
> *Natalie Babbitt, writer*

Babushka: An Old Russian Folktale, Charles Mikolaycak, author and illustrator, *1984, Russia,* FOLKLORE

Babushka is a proud housekeeper, the best in her Russian village. One night, while she is sweeping the snow from her doorstep, she smells cinnamon and sees a procession coming toward her. Among them are the three wise men, following a star to their King. They ask Babushka to come, but she is too busy with her housework. Only later does she regret her decision and set out to find them. She grows old, but she never gives up, and in time she becomes a myth herself: "So on and on, day after day, today and forever, Babushka continues her search. A baby laughs, the smell of cinnamon fills the room, and a tiny gift appears. We know, and we will always know, that Babushka has been there, Babushka who is still seeking the child who was born a King."

Berta Benz and the Motorwagen, Mindy Bingham, illustrated by Itoko Maeno, *1989, Germany,* BIOGRAPHICAL FICTION

By 1888, Karl Benz had designed a "motorwagen," a motorized vehicle that could operate without the aid of a horse. The idea was revolutionary, but marketing it was a real problem—until Karl Benz's wife, Berta, decided to take her two sons on a sixty-mile cross-country trip. The expedition is full of technical difficulties, but Berta solves each one with imagination (and sometimes her garter belt). Once she reaches her destination, she spends the next week touring the countryside, drawing crowds wherever she goes. The trip is a rousing success. Younger children may have some difficulty following the story, but older children, and particularly those interested in cars, will enjoy this portrait of an enterprising woman and her place in history at a moment of great change.

A Birthday Basket for Tia, Pat Mora, illustrated by Cecily Land, *1992, United States,* FICTION

It's the day of great-aunt Tia's surprise ninetieth birthday party. Excited Cecilia and her cat, Chica, look around and wonder what to give Tia. Then Cecilia comes upon the perfect idea—a basket of memories. Into the basket goes the book they read together, a bowl for when they cook, a flowerpot from the kitchen window. Even with the cat getting in Cecilia's way, the basket is soon full. After her nap, Cecilia helps her mom fill the piñata, decorate with balloons, and greet the friends and family who arrive. It's quite a celebration for all, and Tia ends up surprising Cecilia. Brightly colored paper-cuts depict the festivities and generously capture the special connection between Cecilia and her Tia.

A Birthday for Frances, Russell Hoban, illustrated by Lillian Hoban, *1968, United States,* FICTION

The Frances the badger series has won the love and admiration of both children and adults. With her direct and often humorous style, Frances finds her way through a variety of issues, from eating habits, to friendships, to that dreaded moment of bedtime. In *A Birthday for Frances*, she has to deal with the confusing feelings of sibling rivalry. Tomorrow is baby sister Gloria's birthday, and Frances is not very happy about the celebration. Pouting in the broom closet, she laments to her imaginary friend: "That is how it is, Alice. Your birthday is always the one that is not now." Frances does eventually spend two allowances on a gift for Gloria, but parting with the gift becomes its own challenge. Warm pencil illustrations capture the many moods of Frances, and the conversational flow of the story makes for enjoyable reading aloud. And in the end, with some guidance from her parents, it is Frances's decision that makes her a proud little badger.

> *It's such a wonderful feeling to watch a child discover that reading is a marvelous adventure rather than a chore.*
> *Zilpha Keatley Snyder, writer*

Born in the Gravy, Denys Cazet, author and illustrator, *1993, United States,* FICTION

Margarita enthusiastically tells her Papa all kinds of stories about her first day in kindergarten. Some kids cried when their mothers left the classroom; some of the mothers cried too. The nice teacher had them singing, drawing pictures, learning about colors. One boy climbed a tree, another got beans stuck up his nose, and Margarita made a new friend. As Margarita tells her many tales, Papa often responds in Spanish—and no translation is needed. Complete with colorful, expressive crayon drawings, Margarita's very busy day is humorous and reassuring.

Brave Irene, William Steig, author and illustrator, *1986, Europe,* FICTION

Irene's mother, Mrs. Bobbin, has finished the duchess's dress just in time for tonight's ball. Unfortunately, Mrs. Bobbin is sick, so Irene offers to take the dress to the castle. It's a cold winter day made worse by snow and wind. Irene and the wind argue with each other; the wind tells Irene to go home and Irene refuses, determined to complete her important mission. Even when the wind picks up the box and blows the dress out of it, Irene does not give up. A suspenseful tale of courage, *Brave Irene* is fun to read aloud, and is a good silent reader for older children.

The Cherry Tree, Ruskin Bond, illustrated by Allan Eitzen, *1988, India,* FICTION

This quiet story and its illustrations take the reader through the years in a young girl's life as she plants and nurtures a young cherry tree. In Rakhi's Himalayan home, trees are rare and cherry trees are almost nonexistent. Rakhi takes good care of her seedling, watering it and keeping away caterpillars. Accidents still happen: a goat eats the leaves one year; later, a runaway cart breaks the young tree in half. The tree persists, and finally Rakhi is rewarded by the first blossoms, then the first, bitter cherry. By the time Rakhi is eleven, she has grown and so has her tree. The branches now spread wide and strong, and the fruit is plentiful. The simple text of this story holds deeper meanings about growing up amid life's hardships, cycles, and rewards.

> *There is no frigate like a book/To take us lands away.*
> Emily Dickinson, *poet*

China's Bravest Girl: The Legend of Hua Mu Lan, Charlie Chin, illustrated by Tomie Arai, *1993, China,* POETRY

Based on a Chinese poem recorded between A.D. 960 and 1279, *China's Bravest Girl* is a tale of family, honor, and heroics. Young Hua Mu Lan reads a notice from the Emperor declaring that a male from every household must help fight an enemy invasion. Hua Mu Lan goes to her elderly father and says: "I am young and healthy, / and you have no eldest son. / If the Emperor needs a soldier, / then I must be the one." She prepares for her trip, dresses as a man, and leaves her village for war. For ten years she fights and wins many battles, and when she returns home with the rank of a general her family welcomes her with much pride. The rich, colorful illustrations of Tomie Arai reinforce the emotion this book inspires and complement the poetry written in English as well as Chinese characters.

Chinye: A West African Folktale, Obi Onyefulu, illustrated by Evie Safarewicz, *1994, Nigeria,* FOLKLORE

Around the world, stories abound about wicked stepmothers who favor their lazy, natural-born daughters over their hardworking stepchildren. In this West African version, a young girl named Chinye is sent by her stepmother to fetch water from the stream at night. Chinye is terrified, but the usually dangerous forest animals are good to her, and an old woman tells her of a hut filled with gourds. Chinye follows the old woman's advice: she takes home the smallest gourd, smashes it, and finds herself surrounded by treasure. Her greedy stepmother sends off her daughter Nkechi to try her luck, but with disastrous results. The lessons of obedience, true affection, and selflessness are universal; Evie Safarewicz's watercolors make the story geographically specific by taking us to a Nigeria of bright daylight colors and eerie nighttime forests.

Chita's Christmas Tree, Elizabeth Fitzgerald Howard, illustrated by Floyd Cooper, *1989, United States,* BIOGRAPHICAL FICTION

To write this book, Elizabeth Howard drew on her memories of her cousin, the only child of one of Baltimore's first black physicians. It is a gentle, nostalgic book that evokes Chita's life in the early twentieth century: visiting patients in a horse-drawn carriage, making Christmas cookies, buying waffles from the waffle man on the corner, and picking out little Chita's own special Christmas tree. The memories are happy ones, and the illustrations glow with warm oranges and browns, interspersed with the vivid pink or red of a muffler and the bright green of a garland of pine boughs.

> *There is more treasure in books than in all the pirates' loot on Treasure Island.*
>
> *Walt Disney, filmmaker*

Cinder Edna, Ellen Jackson, illustrated by Kevin O'Malley, *1994, United States,* FICTION

Step aside, Cinderella, and meet your neighbor, Cinder Edna. Sure, she has to do all the work for her stepmother and stepsisters, and of course she is not expected to go to the ball, but Cinder Edna is a very resourceful gal; she earns money mowing lawns and cleaning birdcages. Although people may not call her a beauty, this girl is "strong and spunky and [knows] some good jokes." On the evening of the ball, she takes her dress out of layaway, slips on loafers she knows will be comfortable for dancing, and boards the bus for the castle—no fairy godmother for her. The humorous illustrations that surround the story add to its delight. *Cinder Edna* is a great spoof; kids familiar with Cinderella will get a laugh out of this contemporary setting of an ancient story.

The Country Bunny and the Little Gold Shoes, As Told to Jenifer, Du Bose Heyward, illustrated by Marjorie Flack, *1939, United States,* FANTASY

Written in 1939, this feminist classic is bound to delight and inspire mothers and children alike. In her youth, the brown-skinned country bunny's aspiration is to be one of the five Easter Bunnies, but the rich white bunnies and the tall jackrabbits always laugh at her. After she marries and has twenty-one children, the country bunny's fate seems sealed. Or is it? It turns out motherhood has helped her become one of the five wisest, and kindest, and swiftest bunnies in the world. And because she has taught her children to be responsible, she is able to do her job beautifully. The wise and intimate voice of the narrator gives the book a sense of humor that sparkles even as it imparts important lessons.

The Crane Girl, Veronika Martenova Charles, author and illustrator, *1992, Japan,* FOLKLORE

Yoshiko lives by the sea. She and her mother walk the beach during the day, and she and her father play together when he comes home from fishing. All of that changes when her brother, Katsumi, is born. Now Yoshiko feels unhappy and unloved; she wants to be a baby again. At the beach she asks the cranes if she can be their baby, then falls asleep in the grass. The cranes take pity on the lonely child, and when she awakens, Yoshiko is a baby crane. Time passes and one day, when Yoshiko flies over her parents' home, she hears them tell Katsumi about their precious firstborn. Yoshiko decides she must find a way to tell them who she is. The lovely illustrations enhance the emotion of this tender story, and the final pages are filled with joy as Yoshiko and Katsumi dance for the cranes together.

The Crane Wife, Sumiko Yagawa, illustrated by Suekichi Akaba, *1979, Japan,* FOLKLORE

One of Japan's best-loved folktales, *The Crane Wife* is a story of contentment and greed. One winter day, Yohei, a kind but poor peasant farmer, finds a wounded crane. Gently, Yohei tends to the crane's wound. That night a young woman knocks at Yohei's hut and asks to be his wife. Soon the hut becomes a happy home for both of them. As the food stored for winter runs low, the young woman offers to weave some cloth to sell so they can buy food; she asks only that Yohei not watch her. The third time she has to weave cloth, Yohei can no longer contain his curiosity. It is then that Yohei sees his wife's sacrifice and loses her. The watercolor illustrations capture the spareness of winter and Yohei's life, the warmth that can happen when people share, and the sadness caused by Yohei's lack of trust.

Not too long ago, nor far away, where spirits live in the trees and rocks and in the animals that roam at night, there was a bright and pretty girl named Osa who was so afraid of the dark . . .
from Darkness and the Butterfly *by Ann Grifalconi*

Darkness and the Butterfly, Ann Grifalconi, author and illustrator, *1987, Africa,* FICTION

Poor little Osa, smallest of the small. During the day, she is brave and quick, exploring the hills and valleys around her African village. But at night, she is scared of all that she can't see. One day she meets a wise woman, who teaches her about the courage of butterflies, and Osa learns to find her own light in the darkness. A reassuring story, with vibrant illustrations that flow around the words, it reminds us that children all over the world share certain fears—and ways of overcoming them.

Don't Forget, Patricia Lakin, illustrated by Ted Rand, *1994, United States,* FICTION

Tomorrow is Mama's birthday, and eight-year-old Sarah is going to bake her an orange sponge cake. With her list in hand, she stops at the greengrocer's for an orange and at the baker's for flour, and each shop owner gives her a special secret to use in making the perfect cake. Although she wishes she didn't have to, Sarah goes to the Singers' store for the rest of the ingredients. The Singers are nice, but Sarah is afraid of the numbers that are tattooed on their arms, numbers they got while in a concentration camp. It is at the Singers', however, that Sarah learns an important lesson about not forgetting, both about history and baking a cake. Ted Rand's illustrations set the stage of a postwar Jewish neighborhood and illuminate Sarah's excitement and pride. For aspiring bakers, the book concludes with a recipe for Sarah's orange sponge cake.

Dumpling Soup, Jama Kim Rattigan, illustrated by Lillian Hsu-Flanders, *1993, United States,* FICTION

What's better than the combination of food, families, love, and holidays? *Dumpling Soup* draws from Jama Rattigan's childhood memories of New Year's celebrations in Hawaii. Marisa is seven and is being allowed to participate for the first time in making dumplings for the traditional New Year's soup. Of course, her dumplings aren't perfect like her aunts', and of course everyone loves them just the same, but what's really important in this book is the joyous sense of family warmth and tradition that shines off the watercolor pages. As they wait for midnight, we see all the cousins playing "shoe store" with the many pairs of shoes left outside the front door, or lining up for an even better game, "hug grandma." And when the fireworks go off at midnight, the happiness is infectious.

Elinda Who Danced in the Sky: An Eastern European Folktale from Estonia, Lynn Moroney, illustrated by Veg Reisberg, *1990, Estonia,* FOLKLORE

Elinda came from a tiny bird's egg, and her job is to help the birds on their migratory flights. She is beautiful and many wish to marry her, but she turns them all down. Her suitor the Moon has too narrow a path; the Sun is too bright and she would always live in his shadow. But when Prince Borealis comes, Elinda knows she has found a true match. When they are not allowed to marry, she finds her own place in the sky, where her veil becomes the Milky Way, the Moon and the Sun are her friends, and every once in a while, she still can dance with the Aurora Borealis. The story carries with it the soothing and enchanting rhythms of folktales, the messages are positive ones, and the illustrations capture the imagination with their delightful stylized borders and bright colors.

> *I like Eloise! She was* not *a good girl!*
>
> *Hannah Ricketts, age 6*

Eloise, Kay Thompson, illustrated by Hilary Knight, *1955, United States,* FICTION

Oh, that Eloise, she is one rich little troublemaker—so why do so many of us like her and delight in the utter mischief she creates? She zooms through the Plaza Hotel like a whirlwind on roller skates, making chaos out of catering, the switchboard, the mail room, the lobby. She runs her nanny ragged and drives her tutor to distraction.

She imagines scenarios that make your eyes pop out (and you will certainly run out of breath before you get to the end of her stories). Room service must be ready to hang her by her toes. Yet her charm is infectious, and if she's not adorable, she is certainly awe-inspiring.

Emerald Blue, Anne Marie Linden, illustrated by Katherine Doyle, *1994, Barbados,* MEMOIR

When Anne Marie Linden was still young, she left Barbados and the care of her grandmother and moved to the United States to be with her mother. *Emerald Blue* is a loving evocation of Anne Marie's early years, brought to life by Katherine Doyle's gorgeous oil pastels that emanate heat, color, joy, and a tropical sensuality so dense you can almost taste it. In the Barbados of Anne Marie's childhood, goats produce rich, warm milk, and cool grass provides respite from the hot road for the bare feet of brightly clad, exuberant schoolgirls. When Grandmother sighs "Chile . . ." "it was like the soft kiss of the evening breeze." But when her mother comes to fetch her, the excited little girl thinks only of seeing snow, and doesn't realize she is leaving Barbados forever. Expressing gratitude through remembrance, this book becomes a love letter to one grandmother and a way of life.

> *H'man, that gator was thinking he was gonna have a good meal tonight. But Feliciana Feydra felt her pecan baby doll in her hand, and had another thought in mind.*
>
> *from* Feliciana Feydra LeRoux *by Tynia Thomassie*

Feliciana Feydra LeRoux, Tynia Thomassie, illustrated by Cat Bowman Smith, *1995, United States,* FICTION

Feliciana Feydra LeRoux is a tall tale chockful of alligators, adventure, and a quick-thinking, obstinate heroine. It's a natural readaloud, told in a tongue-tingling Cajun dialect—which may take some practice if you're not fluent, but once you've got it, everybody has a blast. Feliciana is the youngest in her clan, Grampa Baby's "teetsie-walla." He'll do anything for her, except take her alligator hunting. Well, ain't nothin' gonna stop Feliciana Feydra LeRoux. She steals her brother's boat, grabs her precious pecan baby doll, and sets off to find herself a "halligator"—and it's a good thing for both her and Grampa that she does. When Feliciana returns home in the back of the big red truck, straddling a huge alligator, she is one happy kid, complete with red armadillo boots, high-flying pigtails, and a big, big grin.

Flicka, Ricka, Dicka and Their New Friend, Maj Lindman, author and illustrator, *1942, Sweden,* FICTION

Flicka, Ricka, and Dicka, the stars of a series of stories, are three blond-haired, blue-eyed little Swedish sisters. In this book, they meet their new neighbor, a grouchy old man, and through their sweet natures and three large pink-and-white lollipops, they make a friend. It turns out the neighbor isn't grouchy at all; he asks them in and teaches them geography, and finally goes sledding with them. The day ends nicely, with a friendship well established. A sweet book, it reminds children to look beyond first impressions and to reach out to those who may be lonely.

Flossie & the Fox, Patricia C. McKissack, illustrated by Rachel Isadora, *1986, United States,* FOLKLORE

In this takeoff on the Little Red Riding Hood story, young Flossie Finley outsmarts the sly fox and delivers her basket of eggs to Miz Viola intact. Flossie is wonderfully unflappable and sure of herself; she simply refuses to believe the fox is a fox. She has him attempting to convince her all the way through the woods: "I aine never seen a fox before. So, why should I be scared of you and I don't even now know you a real fox for a fact?" He has a tail? Well, so does a squirrel, and so on . . . Flossie's spunk and language are contagious and the illustrations practically glow—just wait till you see the sparkling satisfaction on Flossie's face on the last page.

Fox Song, Joseph Bruchac, illustrated by Paul Morin, *1993, United States,* BIOGRAPHICAL FICTION

Jamie is lying awake on her bed, but she doesn't want to open her eyes. She's afraid if she does, she'll lose the picture in her mind of her recently deceased great-grandma. So Jamie spends time with her conscious dreams and remembers the stories Grama told her. Grama had a quick smile and a generous way of teaching. She taught Jamie to thank the birch tree for a piece of its blanket and then to make a basket from it, to see the woods in different ways, and to sing a welcoming song to the new day: "When you sing it, you will not be alone." Paul Morin's rich, warm illustrations provide sympathy for Jamie's sadness and show the humor and love between these two. Joseph Bruchac grew up with his Abenaki grandmother, and in remembering her stories, he shares her caring and giving nature.

Books are the quietest and most constant of friends; they are the most accessible and wisest counsellors, and the most patient of teachers.

Charles W. Eliot, educator

A Gift for Tia Rosa, Karen T. Taha, illustrated by Dee deRosa, *1986, United States,* FICTION

When Tia Rosa comes home from the hospital, her next-door neighbor, Carmela, is overjoyed. She has missed her friend and is anxious to show her the scarf she is knitting. After all, Tia Rosa taught Carmela how to knit and now that Carmela is almost done, Tia Rosa is going to help her with the fringe. For one week they knit together; eight-year-old Carmela works on the scarf, and Tia Rosa on a blanket for her unborn grandchild. Unfortunately, Tia Rosa is very sick and her death deeply saddens young Carmela. Karen Taha's writing allows for Carmela's joy in her friendship and the hurt and confusion Tia Rosa's death brings her. Dee deRosa's illustrations capture both the love and the grief Carmela experiences.

The beauty of this story is the gift of knitting that Tia Rosa gives Carmela and how Carmela uses this gift to aid in her healing and to pay tribute to Tia Rosa.

The Girl Who Loved Caterpillars, Jean Merrill, illustrated by Floyd Cooper, *1992, Japan,* FOLKLORE

The Girl Who Loved Caterpillars, adapted from a twelfth-century Japanese scroll, is a wonderful tale of a clever girl who knows what is important to her and what's not. Izumi loves the natural world; when she is expected to pluck her eyebrows, she refuses; instead "she let her brows grow full and hairy as a caterpillar's back." Although she is a member of upper-class society, she is most comfortable with the street boys who collect caterpillars for her. Her family is embarrassed by her fascination with insects and worried about her marriage prospects. When a nobleman stops by her window, fascinated, she's not whisked off to a married life, however; they have a pleasant exchange, and as he leaves, she is already searching for more caterpillars to study. The richly colored illustrations show an Izumi comfortable with both nature and herself.

The Girl Who Loved Wild Horses, Paul Goble, author and illustrator, *1978, United States,* FOLKLORE

Paul Goble's use of bold, stylized drawings and pure colors absorb the reader in this folktale of a Native American girl who loves horses. As she spends time with the horses of her tribe—knowing the grass they like to eat, tending to any that are injured—the people realize that "she understood horses in a special way." One afternoon, while she sleeps in a meadow, a storm rumbles across the sky. She awakens, surrounded by stampeding, frightened horses; jumping on the back of one, she tries to stop them, but her voice is lost in the wind. They finally outrun the storm, but the girl knows they are now lost. After a year of living with the horses, she comes home, but it is obvious she longs to be running with them again. With celebration, she rejoins the horses, and to this day, the people are happy to know that they have a relative among the wild horses.

The Girl Who Swam with the Fish: An Athabascan Legend, Michelle Renner, illustrated by Christine Cox, *1995, United States,* FOLKLORE

For the young Athabascan girl in this story, summertime means the running of the king salmon that help sustain her family during the winter. Anxiously she watches for them at the river's edge, wondering what it would be like to travel in the water. When she spots the fish, she falls into the river in her excitement and then realizes she has become a young salmon. Although she misses her family, she is happy and heads out to a great ocean with the newly hatched fish and sees many strange and wonderful sights. But what she remembers most is how the fish like to be treated by the humans—with clean drying racks and sharp knives, and their skin turned side-up when it rains. Years pass and the girl-fish returns to her village. Leaping up at the sight of her family, she becomes human again. She teaches her people to respect the salmon; the people listen, and always the salmon return. The girl's round cheeks, the swirl of the water, and her return home remind readers of nature's cycles.

> *A fairy tale . . . demands of the reader total surrender; so long as he is in its world, there must be for him no other. . . . The way, the only way, to read a fairy tale is to . . . throw yourself in. There is no other way.*
>
> *W. H. Auden, writer*

The Girl Who Wanted to Hunt: A Siberian Folktale, Emery Bernhard, illustrated by Durga Bernhard, *1994, Russia,* FOLKLORE

When Anga is young, her father makes her toys, miniatures of the domestic tools she will use later as a woman. She thanks him, but asks for hunting toys: "When I grow up I will be a hunter like you." Although Anga's mean and lazy stepmother disagrees, Anga's father makes her weapons. When Anga's father dies, her stepmother becomes even crueler. Even with the aid of magical animals, Anga cannot keep her happy. Finally, in fear for her life, Anga runs to the Moon, which will always protect her. It is said that you can still see her there "if you open your eyes when the Moon shines its soft silvery light on you." The illustrations frame the words and evoke the traditions and feelings of life in Siberia long ago.

The Goat in the Rug, Charles L. Blood and Martin Link, illustrated by Nancy Winslow Parker, *1976, United States,* FICTION

What a delightful way to learn about Navajo weaving—through the eyes of the goat whose wool is used to make the rug. Glenmae is the weaver and Geraldine is her goat. With Geraldine close by her side, Glenmae clips, washes, cards, spins, collects plants for the dyes, and eventually weaves Geraldine's wool into a beautiful, one-of-a-kind rug. Geraldine is a goat with a sense of humor who narrates and eats her way through the story. Make sure to give children time to look and laugh at the humorous illustrations that accompany this fine tale.

> *[My mother] read to me from the time I was a baby, and once, when I was three or four and she was reading my favorite story, the words on the page, her spoken words, and the scenes in my head fell together in a blinding flash. I could read!*
>
> Trina Schart Hyman, *illustrator and writer*

Gracias, Rosa, Michelle Markel, illustrated by Diane Paterson, *1995, United States and Guatemala,* FICTION

Kate is upset when her new baby-sitter, Rosa, comes to her house. Kate misses her old sitter and isn't sure about this woman who speaks Spanish. But generous Rosa gives Kate a cloth doll from her Guatemalan homeland, and it isn't long before they are friends and Kate is learning some Spanish. As Rosa learns more English, she is able to tell Kate about her family's farm in Guatemala. Rosa talks about her young daughter living in Guatemala and how there is no work in Rosa's village; that's why Rosa is working in the United States. Eventually Rosa goes back to her family, and while Kate will miss her, she gives Rosa a special gift for her daughter.

In *Gracias, Rosa*, Kate's world is broadened through Rosa's love and care, and readers feel a gentle satisfaction when they close the book.

Grandfather's Christmas Camp, Marc McCutcheon, illustrated by Kate Kiesler, *1995, United States,* FICTION

It's Christmas Eve, and Grandfather's three-legged dog, Mr. Biggins, is out somewhere in the snowy wilderness. When Grandfather sets out to find him, Lizzie wants to come, too. So, dressed in umpteen layers of clothes, they head for the top of the mountain. Lizzie gets tired, but you don't complain around Grandfather, even when you end up spending Christmas Eve in a quickly made igloo. There's magic in the night, however, and in the morning, there's Mr. Biggins licking Lizzie's face, and a sled to take them all whizzing home to Grandfather's little cabin in the woods. Kate Kiesler's illustrations capture the snowy cold and the glow of faces and firelight, while Marc McCutcheon creates a dynamic across generations.

Grandmother's Pigeon, Louise Erdrich, illustrated by Jim La Marche, *1996, United States,* FANTASY

"As it turned out, Grandmother was a far more mysterious woman than any of us knew." Oh, the excitement generated by a book that promises much, if only you'll suspend your disbelief. When Grandmother takes off for Greenland riding a porpoise, it's not a shock to her family. The surprise comes later when her two grandchildren enter her room and find pigeon eggs where no live bird has been. The eggs hatch and the birds that appear are identified as an extinct breed of passenger pigeon. The outside world becomes intrigued, but eventually, the children set the birds free—setting in motion events for one more mystery. The wonder of this book is how naturally it integrates fantasy with reality, a porpoise-riding grandmother with a down-to-earth and loving family. The illustrations glow with a beauty that derives its strength from realistic details, right down to the chipped remains of red nail polish on the fingernails of a little girl. Looking at this book, you can believe that magic is a part of everyday life.

How Night Came from the Sea, Mary-Joan Gerson, illustrated by Carla Golembe, *1994, Brazil,* FOLKLORE

Imagine a world without darkness. There is no "sunrise or sunset, starlight or moonbeams . . . no night creatures such as owls or tigers, and no night flowers that secretly open their petals at dusk." A daughter of Iemanja, the goddess of the sea, marries a man of the land, and although she loves her husband and the daylight, in time her heart is filled with longing for darkness. She tells her husband that "night is like the quiet after crying or the end of the storm. It is a dark, cool blanket that covers everything." She knows that darkness is with her mother in the sea. It is then her husband sends three servants into the sea to get a bag of darkness from Iemanja. Bold, brilliant illustrations, with the bluest of skies, the yellowest of suns, and the blackest of skins, contrast and combine, and leave the readers full of appreciation for both the night and the morning star with the roosters crowing.

> *You the reader, aided by your sidekick, are free to do just about anything, changing tempos, cutting lines, adding new ones, departing from the text entirely. As the child's breath thickens and there's a yawn or two, you might wind down to the softest of codas, or end abruptly, leaving the story line hanging at just the right spot, till next time. In short, free improv: reading to kids is to ordinary reading what jazz is to a string quartet.*
>
> *Sean Wilentz, writer*

I Hate English!, Ellen Levine, illustrated by Steve Bjorkman, *1989, United States,* FICTION

Mei Mei "was smart in school. In her school in Hong Kong. In Chinese. But her family moved to New York. She didn't know why. She didn't want to move. And she said all that. In Chinese." Friendly, cartoon watercolors show the reader Mei Mei's new life. She's comfortable in Chinatown, or at the beach with her Chinese friends, but she has difficulty following the lessons in school. To Mei Mei's ears, English is a "lonely language"; the letters, like *t* and *r*, "bang against each other and each keeps its own sound. Not like Chinese." But her English teacher makes a difference. The two go for a walk, and the teacher keeps talking and talking and talking. In English. Until finally, Mei Mei wants to talk. And talk she does. In English. A sweet and energetic book that captures both the richness of Mei Mei's life and her frustrations with her awkward new language, *I Hate English!* is full of insights for both new and native English speakers.

I Have a Sister—My Sister Is Deaf, Jeanne Whitehouse Peterson, illustrated by Deborah Ray, *1977, United States,* AUTOBIOGRAPHY

With pride and poetic language, an older sister tells us about her deaf younger sister. The younger girl plays the piano: "she likes to feel the deep rumbling chords." When the sisters pretend to stalk deer in an empty lot behind their house, the older listens for sounds, the younger looks for movement in the grass. Once, the younger sister made the older take her sunglasses off, causing her to wonder, "What do my brown eyes say to her brown eyes?" Throughout the book, the narrator tells us the things she can do that her sister can't, then tells us all the things that her little sister can do—climb trees, play on the swings—and how she likes the purr of the kitten in her lap and isn't afraid of thunder. The subdued pencil drawings have a quiet strength that show the love and caring between these sisters in this moving celebration of differences.

Imani in the Belly, Deborah M. Newton Chocolate, illustrated by Alex Boies, *1994, East Africa,* FOLKLORE

Imani in the Belly's cut-paper illustrations blast off the pages, spilling their brilliant, highly contrasting colors. Orange gazelles and purple lizards careen across the pages, while Simba, a ferocious black lion with a curling red tongue, stalks villagers who stray beyond the kraal fence. When Simba swallows Imani's children, Imani sets out to get them back, even if it means being eaten herself. Once in the lion's belly, she lights a fire and eventually she, her children, some animals, and many other villagers are coughed back out into the world, to the sound of the villagers' cries of "Faith be to Imani!" This folktale has many variations throughout the world; Deborah Chocolate took inspiration for this version from an 1886 collection of Swahili stories. It's a tale of courage and faith, mother love and quick thinking, made mythical and exciting by the dynamic illustrations.

Imani's Gift at Kwanzaa, Denise Burden-Patmon, illustrated by Floyd Cooper, *1992, United States,* FICTION

Denise Burden-Patmon creates a fluid story line that both describes the African-American celebration of Kwanzaa and draws on the themes of sharing, faith, and creativity that characterize the holiday. Part of a strong and caring family, Imani loves to celebrate Kwanzaa and looks forward to the food, music, and people that fill her house—except when she is told she must be nice to Enna, a new member of a neighborhood family. But when Imani's grandmother reminds her that the first idea of Kwanzaa is Umoja, or unity, she gives Imani something to think about. Lustrous, detailed illustrations evoke the richness of heritage and the warmth of friendship and family.

Jessica, Kevin Henkes, author and illustrator, *1989, United States,* FICTION

Ruthie Simms has no siblings or pets, but she has her best friend Jessica. Wherever Ruthie goes, Jessica goes—to the park, to the moon, to play in the snow. Ruthie always watches out for Jessica; she tells her when the soup is hot, they share books, and are happy and sad together. Ruthie is fine with this arrangement, but her parents, who can't see Jessica, tell Ruthie, "There is no Jessica." Ruthie knows there is. *Jessica* is a delightful tale about an imaginary friend and what happens on the first day of kindergarten.

Reading makes me feel good inside.
    Sarah Maclean, elementary school student

Just Us Women, Jeannette Caines, illustrated by Pat Cummings, *1982, United States,* FICTION

The narrator and her Aunt Martha are going on a trip: "No boys and no men, just us women." They are going to take a picnic, stop at roadside markets and buy whatever they like, and eat peaches from Virginia to North Carolina. If it rains, they'll get out and walk among the raindrops; when their fried chicken runs out, they'll eat in a fancy restaurant. And when they finally arrive and everyone asks them why they took so long, they'll just laugh and tell them, "We had a lot of girl talk to do between the two of us." They have a grand time, and the excitement in their faces is contagious. It makes you want to get out a road map and invite a girl in your life on a nice, long road trip.

Katy and the Big Snow, Virginia Lee Burton, author and illustrator, *1943, United States,* FICTION

"Katy was a beautiful red trawler tractor. She was very big and very strong and she could do a lot of things." She is so big and strong, in fact, that she is called out only for the toughest assignments: "The harder and tougher the job, the better she liked it." So when a snow storm hits the city of Geopolis and all the snow trucks get stuck, it's up to Katy to save the day. Doctors get patients to hospitals, fire trucks arrive at fires, the postmaster gets the mail through, the electric company fixes the power—all following Katy. Virginia Burton, probably best known for *Mike Mulligan and the Steam Shovel*, draws her own illustrations, and children love to trace Katy's trail as she crisscrosses the city and clears all the roads.

The Keeping Quilt, Patricia Polacco, author and illustrator, *1988, United States,* FICTION

When the narrator's great-grandmother came to the United States from Russia, she brought little with her except her blue dress and a bright red babushka. Once the dress is too small, her mother takes pieces of it for a quilt, which is then used as a tablecloth, a wedding huppah, a baby quilt, and finally, when great-grandmother grows old, as a covering for her legs. As the quilt is passed on through successive generations—and becomes again a tablecloth, huppah, baby quilt—some changes occur in the Jewish traditions, but the family draws strength from continuity. The illustrations reinforce this theme; each drawing is done almost entirely in dark browns, set off by the always present red and blue bits of color in the dress and babushka, and then the quilt.

> *When you love someone and they go away, it leaves a hole in you. Even if you know that they'll be coming back, it hurts just the same. This story is for all of you.*
>
> *from* Kisses from Rosa *by Petra Mathers*

Kisses from Rosa, Petra Mathers, author and illustrator, *1995, Germany,* MEMOIR

In 1949, Petra Mathers was sent to her Aunt Mookie in the Black Forest while her mother recovered from tuberculosis. Told from the perspective of a young girl named Rosa, this book recalls both Petra Mathers's pain of separation and the love of relatives and friends. Whimsical illustrations show Rosa as she blossoms under the care of Aunt Mookie and Mother Schmidt. On the farm there are big-eyed cows, blueberries to pick, and always, letters to write and look forward to receiving. One picture shows all of Rosa's different kinds of kisses—Eskimo, bird, butterfly, wet fish, and lion—as they fly on wings to her mother. Just before Christmas, an exuberant Rosa returns home, a little sad to leave the farm, and full to bursting of all the things she has experienced.

The Korean Cinderella, Shirley Climo, illustrated by Ruth Heller, *1993, Korea,* FOLKLORE

Variations of the theme of Cinderella abound in oral and written traditions from around the world, and although the general story line is similar, each offers the distinct flavor of its cultural origin. Shirley Climo's *The Korean Cinderella* combines three Korean variations of this tale while intertwining the spirit world of the culture.

Pear Blossom is the name of this Cinderella, who accomplishes her series of seemingly overwhelming tasks with the aid of a toad, sparrows, and a black bull. The fancy ball here is a local festival and the prince is a magistrate, but you know the rest: the lost sandal, the marriage, and the happily-ever-after lives. Ruth Heller's bold and detailed artwork radiates the feel of that ancient country, captivating the reader and highlighting the sense of drama and setting.

The Legend of the Bluebonnet, Tomie dePaola, author and illustrator, *1993, United States,* FOLKLORE

The Comanche people have a legend that describes how wild lupines came to the area now known as Texas. The story tells of the many people who have died because of drought and famine, including the parents of the young girl She-Who-Is-Alone. The Great Spirits must be appeased in order to bring rain. She-Who-Is-Alone knows her sacrifice must be her doll, her only gift from her parents. Quietly, in a night surrounded by stars, she lights a fire, thinks of her past and of the present, then offers her doll to the Great Spirits. After the fire cools, she spreads the ashes in four directions and falls asleep. In the morning the hillside is covered with bluebonnets and the Comanche people know that it is a sign of forgiveness. The subtle illustrations complement the innate wisdom of She-Who-Is-Alone.

> *Finding the stories, the history, of our past can change our understandings of our identity, our culture and our future.*
>
> *Jesse Larsen, writer and artist*

The Library, Sarah Stewart, illustrated by David Small, *1995, United States,* POETRY

Elizabeth Brown "didn't like to play with dolls, / She didn't like to skate. / She learned to read quite early / And at an incredible rate." In fact, you are lucky if you ever see Elizabeth's lively, bespectacled face, for there is nothing that makes her happier than to have a book right up to her nose. As a consequence, she slips through childhood, ignores dating, and eventually lives in a house that becomes filled to the rafters with books. So what does she do? She donates her home and books to start a free library for her town, and goes to live with a girlfriend. A lighthearted book that celebrates and pokes loving fun at the book-obsessed, it's sure to produce both smiles and empathy.

The Lighthouse Keeper's Daughter, Arielle North Olson, illustrated by Elaine Wentworth, *1987, United States,* HISTORICAL FICTION

The Lighthouse Keeper's Daughter is based on the experiences of several girls who helped their fathers maintain lighthouses along the Maine coast during the 1850s. In this story, young Miranda must keep the lighthouse lamps lit and the windows deiced while her father goes to the mainland for supplies. His overnight trip turns into weeks as winter storms isolate the rocky island where Miranda and her mother wait, their food dwindling. Miranda vigilantly does her job, resolved that no ship will run aground while she is in charge. When Miranda becomes sick, her mother overcomes her own fear of heights and helps Miranda up the long stairway to the top of the lighthouse. Finally, father returns. Word of Miranda's bravery spreads, and brings a lovely, unexpected reward. Watercolor illustrations opposite pages filled with text give depth and detail to this true-to-life tale of courage.

> *In the sudden rush of darkness their diyas glowed—bright, brighter, brightest—filling the living room with light. "We beat the darkness, we beat the darkness!" Gita clapped her hands.*
>
> From Lights for Gita *by Rachna Gilmore*

Lights for Gita, Rachna Gilmore, illustrated by Alice Priestley, *1994, United States,* FICTION

Gita knows that today her extended family back in New Delhi will be celebrating Divali, to honor the Goddess Lakshmi, who brings prosperity and happiness. There will be sweet treats to eat, *diyas*—small clay pots filled with mustard oil—to light, stories to tell, and, best of all, fireworks at night. But this cold, sleety November day makes Gita wish her family had never moved to the United States. Because of the weather, her school friends can't come to her Divali party, and when the power goes out, poor Gita is heartbroken. It is then, with her mother's help, that Gita comes to understand that Divali is really about "filling the darkness with light. . . . We must do it ourselves." With her home glowing from the light of the *diyas* and with the surprise arrival of a friend who lives near enough to come to the celebration, Gita realizes that although Divali is different in her new home, the reasons for it remain the same.

Little Wynne's Giggly Thing, Laurel Dee Gugler, illustrated by Russ Willms, *1995, Canada,* FICTION

Little Wynne lives with Molly, Kim, and Jeri, three very hard-working adults. In fact, it seems they never stop: Molly works in the garden, Kim bakes "the fluffiest bread in town," and Jeri keeps the house spotless. Little Wynne likes to invent things, but it seems no one appreciates them. Sadly, Little Wynne puts her jingly thing and cuddly thing inventions in the closet. When Wynne makes her giggly thing, however, she decides she won't hide it no matter what. Through her persistence, her creation gets the whole household laughing, and you know what? "After that, giggles often rippled through the house, and, it is said, the vegetables grew even bigger, the bread rose higher, and the floors were shinier." Off-the-wall illustrations punctuated with big, wide grins add to the energy of this book. Know any type-A parents who need a good giggle?

Liza Lou and the Yeller Belly Swamp, Mercer Mayer, author and illustrator, *1976, United States,* FANTASY

Liza Lou has her hands full. Her mother keeps sending her across the swamp with provisions for various friends and neighbors, but everybody knows that swamp is full of hideous witches, haunts, and gobblygooks—so what's a girl to do? Well, Liza Lou is fearless and smart as a whip, and one by one she outwits those bad creatures until there are none left. Mercer Mayer's language is boisterous—perfect for reading aloud—and the cartoon-style illustrations contrast spunky little Liza Lou with some perfectly dreadful adversaries.

Lottie's Dream, Bonnie Pryor, illustrated by Mark Graham, *1992, United States,* FICTION

Lottie grows up far away from the ocean, yet it fills her dreams. As a young pioneer, she moves to Kansas, where the only sea is made of grass. She grows up, meets Indians, fights winter storms, and eventually marries and has children of her own. One year, as a birthday present, her husband takes her on a trip to see the ocean: "She fell asleep to the tune of the pounding surf and knew she was home." Later, widowed, Lottie decides to return to the seashore to live. This is a book about having a dream, even if it has no relation to the life you are living, and realizing that dream, even if it takes a long, long time. It's a grown-up message, presented in an accessible way, with lovely paintings by Mark Graham.

> *Books are fragile, rare treasures that belong to many, many people.*
>
> *Sundaira Morninghouse, writer*

The Lotus Seed, Sherry Garland, illustrated by Tatsuro Kiuchi, *1993, Vietnam and United States,* FICTION

The simple text and strong illustrations of *The Lotus Seed* combine to tell a powerful story. As a child living in Vietnam, a girl sees the Emperor cry when he loses his throne and she saves a lotus seed as a reminder of that tragic event. She takes special care of the seed and when she is forced to leave Vietnam, the seed comes to the United States with her. Now, many years later, her granddaughter tells us the stories of the seed. Through them we learn how something as tiny as a seed can mean so much, and can pass on both history and family heritage.

Lucy's Picture, Nicola Moon, illustrated by Alex Ayliffe, *1994, England,* FICTION

Lucy's very excited; her grandfather is coming for a visit and she is making him a picture at school. It's not a painting-picture, however; Lucy digs through the art-supply box and picks out a green velvet for the hills and a smooth blue fabric for a lake. Outside on the playground she collects twigs, feathers, leaves, and sand. Back in the classroom, surrounded by all the materials she has gathered, Lucy creates her artwork: a collage of Grandpa's farm. Illustrator Alex Ayliffe, herself a collage artist, uses bright, primary colors to evoke the feeling of a collage, while at the same time re-creating the imaginative messiness that occurs with young children and artwork. And when Lucy's grandfather arrives, he comes with his seeing-eye dog, for Lucy's grandfather is blind and he sees her picture with his hands.

The Magic Feather, Lisa Rojany, illustrated by Philip Kuznicki, *1995, Jamaica,* FOLKLORE

The myth of the mancrow came to Jamaica from West Africa. Half-animal, half-human, the mancrow can steal the colors from the world, and keeps his magic in one colored feather in his tail. When he takes the light from Solidae's world and the plants begin to die, Solidae decides it is up to her to bring the colors back. Through illustrations that resemble bold and fantastical stained-glass windows, the mancrow becomes a huge presence, with dark, jagged wings, a screaming yellow beak, and glaring red eyes. Solidae, by contrast, appears an unlikely adversary—a slim, brown-skinned little girl in a cheerful red-and-yellow dress. Yet with flattery, wit, and the help of the animals, she captures the mancrow and yanks out his magic feather, and daylight and color flood back into the world.

Many Moons, James Thurber, illustrated by Marc Simont, *1943, Europe,* FICTION

Princess Lenore is sick from "a surfeit of raspberry tarts." She is sure if she can get the moon, she will recover. None of the king's advisors can help him get Lenore the moon, although they are more than eager to list the many (and often humorous) things they have obtained or accomplished for him. No, they tell the king, the moon is too big, too heavy. It cannot be gotten. It is the Court Jester who comes up with the unique idea of asking Lenore how big and far away the moon is. For Lenore, the moon is only as big as her thumbnail, and only as far away as the branches of her tree. And, of course, it is made of gold. Soon Lenore has a little gold moon on a necklace and all is well—until the king realizes that the next night the moon will rise again. How to explain why Lenore has one moon while another rests in the sky? Everyone is in a tizzy until the Court Jester comes up with the unique idea of asking Lenore . . . James Thurber, a wise and funny man, reminds us that often, to understand how children think, all you need to do is ask them.

> [I]n reading . . . stories, you can be many different people in many different places, doing things you would never have a chance to do in ordinary life. It's amazing that those twenty-six little marks of the alphabet can arrange themselves on the pages of a book and accomplish all that. Readers are lucky—they will never be bored or lonely.
>
> Natalie Babbitt, writer

Maria Molina and the Days of the Dead, Kathleen Krull, illustrated by Enrique O. Sanchez, *1994, Mexico and United States,* FICTION

The Days of the Dead are an important holiday in Mexico; they both honor people who have died and celebrate life. Maria and her family go to the graveyard on October 31 to honor Pablo, her baby brother. With them they bring his favorite toys, special bread, and a sugar-candy skull with his name on it. The next night they remember her grandmother. There is a fiesta; people sing and dance, and there are fireworks all night long. By the following year, Maria and her family have moved to the United States. On October 31, Maria trick-or-treats for Halloween, but worries about Pablo's and Abuela's spirits until her parents show her how they will carry on the tradition here in their new homeland. With an accessible, informative writing style and subdued yet colorful illustrations, the magic of the Days of the Dead fiesta rises from the pages.

Masai and I, Virginia Kroll, illustrated by Nancy Carpenter, *1992, East Africa and United States,* FICTION

In school, a little girl learns about "a tall, proud people called the Masai. I feel the tingle of kinship flowing through my veins." Throughout the day, the girl considers her own life, and how it is different from that of a Masai girl. She knows some of the people in her apartment building, but if she were Masai, she would know everyone in the village; she goes to the corner deli, but her counterpart follows a honey guide bee and gathers her own treat. Even across the ocean and continents, however, some things stay the same. The illustrations in this graceful, proud book reinforce the theme of commonality; initially the two cultures are presented on opposing pages, but as the text moves toward similarities, the pictures begin to merge.

The Maybe Garden, Kimberly Burke-Weiner, illustrated by Fredrika P. Spillman, *1992, United States,* FICTION

The narrator is going to plant a garden and Mother has practical suggestions—marigolds, maybe, to keep the snails away. But this child has opinions, and imagines a garden where snails, bunnies, deer, even bears are welcome. A row of poppies turns into a rainbow of flowers, complete with lanterns because "I've never seen a rainbow at night." The gardens, real and imaginary, are depicted through lush oil pastels, bursting with color, rough on the edges. The illustrations were purposefully designed to present an androgynous child—you and your young one get to decide whether this budding gardener with short blond hair, blue shorts, and white T-shirt is a girl or boy. All things are possible in this creative, inspiring story.

> *My mother has the most immaculate garden in the world. Yet mine is the most enchanting.*
> *from* The Maybe Garden *by Kimberly Burke-Weiner*

May'naise Sandwiches & Sunshine Tea, Sandra Belton, illustrations by Gail Gordon Carter, *1994, United States,* FICTION

Big Mama and her granddaughter like to look through the pictures in Big Mama's scrapbook while she tells stories. One picture prompts memories of a childhood friend, Bettie Jean, who lived in the affluent black section of town. The first time Bettie Jean came over to play, Big Mama begged her mother to make something special for a picnic lunch. Her mother brought out may'naise sandwiches and sugar water, which she called sunshine tea, and Bettie Jean was entranced. Later that night, Big Mama's father told her something she remembered all her life: "Nothing shameful 'bout sometimes havin' food that's kinda thin on fixings, Little Miss. . . . The important thing is to use those thin fixings to help you imagine a full-up plate. . . . It's a fact that those thin fixings can make you determined to get a plate that's piled high." Big Mama's pride in her own college graduation picture reinforces the lesson her granddaughter quickly takes to heart.

The Miracle of the Potato Latkes: A Hanukkah Story, Malka Penn, illustrated by Giora Carmi, *1994, Russia,* FOLKLORE

Every year at Hanukkah, Tante Golda takes eight potatoes and makes crispy, golden latkes for eight of her friends and neighbors. They tell her not to use up her potatoes, but she always answers that God will provide, and somehow, she always makes it through the winter, with help here and there from her neighbors. One year, however, no one has potatoes, and Tante Golda is facing a sad Hanukkah. When a beggar comes to her door, she makes latkes with her last potato. But then a strange thing happens, and continues to happen for each of the next seven days of Hanukkah. Echoing the original Hanukkah story, this is a lovely tale of miracles, faith, and giving.

Mirette on the High Wire, Emily Arnold McCully, author and illustrator, *1992, France,* FICTION

The setting is nineteenth-century Paris. Mirette's home is in her mother's boardinghouse, an exciting place where artists, jugglers, and actors live. When the famous tightrope walker Monsieur Bellini comes to stay, Mirette begs him to teach her to walk the wire. Finally, he agrees. It turns out, however, that Bellini no longer walks the wire for crowds; he is afraid. How Mirette helps him overcome his fear makes for a suspenseful story of friendship and courage. Emily McCully's lively illustrations show us the bustling world of nineteenth-century Paris, the view from atop a high wire strung between two tall houses, and brave Mirette, with her long, curling red hair.

> *The only imaginative works we ought to grow out of are those which it would have been better not to have read at all.*
>
> C. S. Lewis, *writer*

Miss Rumphius, Barbara Cooney, author and illustrator, *1982, United States,* FICTION

While still a little girl, Alice Rumphius decides that she wants to travel the world and then live by the sea when she grows old, as did her grandfather. But Grandfather tells her there is another important thing: "You must do something to make the world more beautiful." Alice does travel the world—an extraordinary thing for a woman in the nineteenth century—and she returns to the seaside. But even as an old woman, she is not sure what she can do to make the world more beautiful. Then one day, by chance, she knows. One of the best-loved books by prolific author and illustrator Barbara Cooney, *Miss Rumphius* teaches children about each person's responsibility to make her own small difference in the world.

Miss Tizzy, Libba Moore Gray, illustrated by Jada Rowland, *1993, United States,* FICTION

While everyone else in the neighborhood has "white houses, white fences and very neat flower gardens," Miss Tizzy has a pink house and flowers that invade the sidewalk. An elderly black woman who wears a purple hat and green high-top tennis shoes, she is the favorite of the neighborhood children, who come to her house and bake cookies, create puppet shows, go on parades, draw pictures— you name it. When Miss Tizzy becomes ill, the children miss her, until they come up with their own get-well solution. Brightly colored illustrations share the warmth of the children and the irrepressible Miss Tizzy.

Mufaro's Beautiful Daughters: An African Tale, John Steptoe, author and illustrator, *1987, Zimbabwe,* FOLKLORE

Many cultures have folktales that tell of the triumph of selflessness over selfishness. John Steptoe drew his inspiration for *Mufaro's Beautiful Daughters* from an 1895 collection, *Kaffir Folktales* by G. M. Theal. Lustrous illustrations evoke the abundant countryside of Zimbabwe, the serenity of kind Nyasha, the greed and cruelty of her sister Manyara, and the eeriness of the characters who test the two sisters' true worth as they travel their separate ways to meet the king. Which sister will the king choose for his wife? The answer is a foregone conclusion, made more absorbing by the journey and the experience of stepping into a rich geography and culture.

My Friend Leslie: The Story of a Handicapped Child, Maxine B. Rosenberg, photographs by George Ancona, *1983, United States,* BIOGRAPHY

Karin is anxious to tells us all about her good friend and fellow kindergartner Leslie. Leslie was born with several handicaps. She wears her hearing aids, but she thinks her glasses are a bother. When Karin and Leslie paint, Leslie has to get very close to the paint and her pictures, and often gets paint on her face. Then she puts paint on Karin's face and they laugh together. Leslie's favorite activity is reading; when she reads *Little Red Riding Hood* aloud, her voice goes low for the wolf and high for Red Riding Hood. She is the best in the class, and everyone applauds when she is finished. Leslie sometimes gets frustrated by her handicaps and Karin doesn't always know what to do, but they are friends and they stick by each other. The book is full of photographs that capture their days together, and leave a lasting impression of these ordinary, extraordinary girls.

My Great-aunt Arizona, Gloria Houston, illustrated by Susan Condie Lamb, *1992, United States,* BIOGRAPHY

Gloria Houston's Great-aunt Arizona was born in a log cabin in the Blue Ridge Mountains back when girls wore long, full dresses and high-button shoes. She grew up tapping trees for maple syrup in the winter and catching tadpoles in the summer, and while she dreamed of visiting far-off places, she never did. She read and read about them, and became a schoolteacher in the same one-room schoolhouse where she went to school: "For fifty-seven years my Great-aunt Arizona hugged her students. She hugged them when their work was good and she hugged them when it was not." In the end, the author reminds us that while Great-aunt Arizona didn't explore the world herself, she travels in the minds of those whose lives she touched.

> *My mother would go out in a rowboat with a bunch of books and she would drop anchor and read to us. She often read what she wanted to read and I suppose it was a way of getting her reading time in. But I think she genuinely enjoyed spending this time with us and I realized later just how amazing it was.*
>
> *Nancy Willard, writer*

Nadia the Willful, Sue Alexander, illustrated by Lloyd Bloom, *1983, North Africa,* FICTION

Nadia, the daughter of Sheik Tarik, is a young Bedouin girl with a stubborn will and a quick temper. Only Nadia's beloved brother Hamed can calm her angry outbursts, but one day, Hamed rides out into the desert to find new grazing ground and never returns. A grief-stricken Sheik Tarik proclaims that Hamed's name must never be spoken again. Angered, feeling as if she is losing her brother a second time by not articulating what he brought to her life, Nadia begins to tell stories of Hamed throughout the camp. In this way she keeps her brother's image alive for herself, and eventually for her father as well. While the black-and-white pencil drawings take readers to a land far away, the issues of death, loss, and remembrance are relevant ones for readers around the world.

Nettie's Trip South, Ann Turner, illustrated by Ronald Himler, *1987, United States,* HISTORICAL FICTION

Ann Turner was inspired to write this book after reading her great-grandmother's diary of a trip she took from Albany, New York, to Richmond, Virginia, in 1859. *Nettie's Trip South,* written as a letter from ten-year-old Nettie to her friend, is filled with Nettie's unforgettable images and enhanced by Ronald Himler's powerful pencil drawings. When Nettie sees slaves for the first time, and her sister tells her that according to the Constitution slaves are three-fifths of a person, Nettie can't see what they are missing. At the hotel, Nettie meets a slave who has no last name, "like a cat or a dog." It is when they stop at a slave auction and Nettie sees two children her age get sold to different people, then watches them separated by force, that she throws up. Her trip and all she sees fill her with a raw sense of injustice, and upon her return home she becomes a committed abolitionist.

A New Coat for Anna, Harriet Ziefert, illustrated by Anita Lobel, *1986, Europe,* BIOGRAPHICAL FICTION

In postwar Europe, there is little money and the stores are almost empty. Anna needs a new coat, but how to get one? Anna's resourceful mother comes up with a solution. A gold watch buys the wool from a farmer's sheep, which Anna happily visits all during the winter as she waits for the spring shearing. An old woman gladly takes a lamp in exchange for spinning; wild lingonberries picked by Anna and her mother make a beautiful red dye; and so on. In the end, Anna has a new coat, and she and her mother invite everyone who helped to a Christmas party in their war-torn house. Harriet Ziefert draws the story from the life experience of a real mother and daughter, while Anita Lobel's stylized illustrations celebrate our ability to create amid the destruction of war.

New Shoes for Silvia, Johanna Hurwitz, illustrated by Jerry Pinkney, *1993, South America,* FICTION

Silvia's Tia Rosita sent the family a package with gifts for everyone. Silvia thinks her gift is the best—red shoes with buckles—red as the setting sun, as a watermelon, as a rose. Alas, they are too big. Luscious illustrations take us along as Silvia sleeps with her red shoes or uses them to create doll beds or a two-car train, all the while waiting to grow into them. Through Silvia, the reader experiences life in this unnamed South American village. Papa and the oxen plow the field; a new baby is born; cattle, goats, and cars together roam the village streets. By the end of the story, Silvia does grow into her shoes, then wonders if next time Tia Rosita will send blue ones.

> *Once, far away in another America, a package arrived at the post office.*
>
> *from* New Shoes for Silvia *by Johanna Hurwitz*

The Night the Grandfathers Danced, Linda Theresa Raczek, illustrated by Katalin Olah Ehling, *1995, United States,* FICTION

The Ute people traditionally perform a four-day spring ritual called the Bear Dance. Given her first chance to participate, Autumn Eyetoo excitedly clips her hair into a beaded barrette and puts on her pink shawl—with its fringes she can touch and thus choose a partner for the dance. But the boys all run away when Autumn and her friends come near, and they have no one to dance with until Autumn spots several old men who have sat on the sidelines all day. What happens then is a little bit of real-life magic. The unusual and intricate batik illustrations place deep browns, oranges, and golds against the vivid black of long hair and the pink from a shirt, skirt, or special shawl, as the descriptions evoke the smell of cedar fires and fry bread and the joy of people coming together.

No More Baths, Brock Cole, author and illustrator, *1980, United States,* FICTION

Jessie lives on a farm, and on a farm you can get very dirty. When her mom decides Jessie needs a bath in the middle of the day, it's too much. Jessie decides to run away. Taking cues from the farm animals, she decides to clean herself. She talks with a chicken and tries to learn to frazzle like chickens do, but that doesn't work. Mrs. Cat tells her to lick the palms of her hands and rub her nose and behind her ears, but that just makes Jessie's hair look sticky and tangled. Lying in the mud with Mrs. Pig gets Jessie cold and wet. Eventually Jessie does take a bath—but that doesn't mean she likes it.

Now Everybody Really Hates Me, Jane Read Martin and Patricia Marx, illustrated by Roz Chast, *1993, United States,* FICTION

Patty Jane Pepper has been sent to her room for hitting her younger brother at his birthday party. She didn't hit him, she just touched him hard, and besides, she only wanted "to look at his new dump truck for one measly second." Alone in her room, she decides she will never come out, speak in a language only she understands, and never, ever clean up her room. Off her imagination soars as she pictures herself at forty, and in little Patty Jane's mind, that is old. After not eating "a morsel of food for over 67 minutes," she is coaxed out of her room for ice cream and cake, knowing she can always go back. The hilarious and colorful illustrations capture a spirited Patty Jane, much to the amusement of her readers.

Ntombi's Song, Jenny Seed, illustrated by Anno Berry, *1987, South Africa,* FICTION

Six-year-old, long-limbed Ntombi is a pretty big girl now, big enough to go by herself on an errand to the local rural South African market. When faced with a stretch of road that runs next to the deep, dark forest, however, Ntombi loses some of her confidence. A minor tragedy brings out Ntombi's courage; a further challenge calls on her resourcefulness and talent. In the end, Ntombi is one happy, grown-up little girl. Although everyone, even young children, might have predicted Ntombi's ultimate success, the unexpected twists throughout the story allow readers to empathize with Ntombi's shifting feelings of self-assurance and uncertainty, and make this a more satisfying and complex reading experience.

On the Pampas, Maria Cristina Brusca, author and illustrator, *1991, Argentina,* AUTOBIOGRAPHICAL FICTION

When Maria Cristina Brusca was a young girl, she spent summers on her grandparents' ranch, La Carlota, in Argentina. Many years later and in appreciation of her time there, she wrote *On the Pampas.* In the book, Maria is greeted by her cousin Susanita, who lives on the ranch year-round. This summer Maria wants to become a gaucho. The girls spend their time with their horses and even swim in the creek with them, holding onto their manes. Maria learns how to use a lasso, and when she herds cattle, she gets to yell louder than she does in the city. In the afternoons, the cousins explore the fields for nandu eggs, relax in the cool of a eucalyptus grove, or take a two-hour ride to the general store. Some evenings they go down to the maté house where the gauchos live and listen to ghost stories. The festive illustrations celebrate the author's memories of this special place and people, and by summer's end, young Maria has indeed become a gaucho.

> *What do we ever get nowadays from reading to equal the excitement and revelation of those first fourteen years?*
>
> Graham Greene, *writer*

One Morning in Maine, Robert McCloskey, author and illustrator, *1952, United States,* FICTION

There's nothing like losing that first tooth—it's an event up there with rocket launches for most children. For Sal, the day is particularly eventful, because after wiggling the tooth all morning, she loses it while digging for clams with her father. Now she has a dilemma: how can she put the tooth under her pillow and make a wish for a chocolate ice-cream cone if she doesn't have the tooth? Maybe wishing on a feather will do. A ride in the motorboat from their island over to town helps dispel her frustration and then—surprise! it all works out. Robert McCloskey's story and pencil drawings show life in one of the more remote areas of Maine in the 1950s, and capture the excitement of one round-nosed, big-eyed little girl, who still believes in wishes and feathers and the thrill of flying across water in a boat.

Owl Moon, Jane Yolen, illustrated by John Schoenherr, *1987, United States,* FICTION

This is a wise and luminous story about a young girl who is going owling for the first time in the woods near her family's Midwestern farm. The girl knows to be silent and brave. She follows sturdily behind her father, experiencing the darkness, her father's owl calls, her feelings of disappointment when she thinks nothing will happen. Suddenly, she is awestruck: the owl is staring at her, caught in the beam of her father's flashlight. Later, as she goes home, she knows she can make noise, but doesn't. She realizes, "When you go owling you don't need words or warm or anything but hope. That's what Pa says. The kind of hope that flies on silent wings under a shining Owl Moon." Award-winning watercolor illustrations match the mood, making this a perfect going-to-bed story.

> *Grandma took part of the pant leg and cut a few squares. Jim gave her a hug and watched her add his patches to the others. "A quilt won't forget. It can tell your life story," she said.*
> *from* The Patchwork Quilt *by Valerie Flournoy*

The Patchwork Quilt, Valerie Flournoy, illustrated by Jerry Pinkney, *1985, United States,* FICTION

Tanya's mother says it's easier to buy a new quilt, but Grandma says she wants to make her own, her masterpiece. Tanya helps

Grandma, and over the course of the next year, Tanya sees favorite bits and pieces of clothes enter into the story of the quilt. When Grandma falls ill, it is Tanya and her mother who keep working on the quilt. Grandma gets better and is able to finish her work, but not before Tanya's family has learned about heritage, remembering, and working together.

The Patient Stone, M. and N. Batmanglij, illustrated by Franta, *1986, Iran,* FOLKLORE

The Patient Stone is the retelling of an ancient Persian folktale about a mythical stone that has the power to listen to people's sorrows and then burst to offer relief and healing. Fahti is a kind, virtuous young girl. When she hears a voice telling her that death is her destiny, Fahti and her parents become frightened and leave their town. Early on, this story becomes a mythical, spiritual journey, and soon Fahti is alone in a mansion in the desert. In one of the rooms lies a young man, with instructions on how to care for him over the next forty days. Fahti faithfully tends to him, only to have her good work foiled by the appearance of another young girl. In this tale, with the aid of the patient stone, Fahti is spiritually rewarded when the truth is revealed. The text, English on one side of the page and Persian on the other, and the colorful, wispy illustrations give this story a feeling of otherworldliness.

Peeping Beauty, Mary Jane Auch, author and illustrator, *1993, United States,* FICTION

In this unabashedly gleeful twist on any number of classic stories and fairy tales, Poulette is an aspiring ballerina, who also happens to be a chicken. When her friends question her chances of success, she responds grandly, "I have to follow my dream." A fox appears on the scene, intent on dinner à la Poulette. Although Poulette is wary, she finally follows him after he promises stardom, audiences, and a gorgeous costume. Soon she learns her mistake. But wait. Poulette is both crafty and strong, and she and her female friends turn the tables on Mr. Fox. The illustrations are bright and witty, as is Poulette, who reminds us: "A fox is still a fox, no matter what he promises. But a talented hen will never be a chicken dinner."

The People Who Hugged the Trees, Deborah Lee Rose, illustrated by Birgitta Saflund, *1990, India,* FOLKLORE

There is a 300-year-old legend from India of a girl named Amrita Devi, who along with several hundred villagers lost her life trying to save the trees near their village from being cut down by the soldiers of the Maharajah. That village is now India's first National Environmental Memorial, and their tradition is carried on in the Chipko ("Hug the Tree") resistance movement. In this softened adaptation of the legend, the Maharajah spares the trees and the villagers after a violent sandstorm convinces him of the trees' importance in protecting the village and its well, but the villagers' courage and devotion to their trees, the role the trees play in their lives, and the reality of living in the desert all come across clear and strong. Intricate, saturated watercolors contrast a harsh desert with stately green trees and a proud, resilient people.

> *There's a pond out back and down the hill from our house. It's too shallow and mucky to swim in. And in August it smells like an old wet mop. But my best friend Carole and I like to play there every day, all year round.*
>
> *from* Pond Year *by Kathryn Lasky*

Pond Year, Kathryn Lasky, illustrated by Mike Bostock, *1995, United States,* FICTION

Pond Year revels in the delight that many children find in the oozy, gooey part of nature. The narrator and her best friend Carole spend lots of time at their pond, catching tadpoles and crawdaddies, finding yellow lady's slippers, making scum wigs for their old baldheaded dolls and friendship rings for each other: "best friends, pond buddies, scum chums forever." There is much to learn from this book and its watercolor illustrations. You follow the pond through the seasons as the scum grows and recedes, the animals change, and two little girls play, explore, and promise each other that next year, when they are seven, they will stay quiet long enough to catch sight of a pond muskrat at night.

The Princess and the Lord of the Night, Emma Bull, illustrated by Susan Gaber, *1994, Europe,* FANTASY

There is a curse on the princess; she must get everything she wants, or the Lord of the Night will destroy her parents' kingdom. "Some people, if they got everything they wanted, would become spoiled and silly before they could turn around once"—except this princess has seen the pressure the curse puts on her parents. So on her thirteenth birthday, she goes off by herself to find the thing she wants, taking with her the gifts she has received in the past: her horse that can cross the kingdom in a day, her crow that can recite all the poetry in the world, her cat "swift as a blink and as clever as six professors," her dog that understands everything she says, and her cloak that makes one invisible. Each gift becomes a gift again, as the princess overcomes the Lord of the Night and gets what she wants in this clever fairy tale of give-and-take.

Punga, the Goddess of Ugly, Deborah Nourse Lattimore, author and illustrator, *1993, New Zealand,* FOLKLORE

On New Zealand's North Island, Grandmother is teaching her twin granddaughters, Maraweia and Kiri, all about Maori ways. If they learn their lessons well, they will earn a fine moko, a chin tattoo. When it is time to practice the haka dance, where you stick out your tongue to show your bravery, Maraweia becomes silly and wants to look ugly. Instead of getting angry, Grandmother tells them the story of Mudfish and Lizard. Long ago, as a result of their silliness and lack of respect for the haka dance, they were captured by Punga, goddess of ugly, and are now stuck on her lodge house. Grandmother then goes to bed, and later that night, the story becomes very real to Kiri and Maraweia. Deborah Lattimore's phenomenal watercolors take you deep into a New Zealand forest. The author's notes and glossary of information about the plants and animals give context to this ancient folk tale.

> *"Kick those legs up," Carrie told her, "and clap your hands. If you gonna dance, girl, you gotta have rhythm."*
> from Ragtime Tumpie *by Alan Schroder*

Ragtime Tumpie, Alan Schroder, illustrated by Bernie Fuchs, *1989, United States,* BIOGRAPHICAL FICTION

Josephine Baker was an amazing woman. She left home at fourteen with almost no money, became a famous honky-tonk dancer and a star in the Ziegfeld Follies, and was awarded medals for her work for the French Resistance during World War II. This fictionalized biography describes moments in one summer when Josephine was a young child. As the paintings draw you into the swirl and shadows of honky-tonk joints and the warm yellows of a St. Louis summer, readers are introduced to Tumpie—a determined little firecracker of a girl whose feet just have to dance.

The Rajah's Rice: A Mathematical Folktale from India, David Barry, illustrated by Donna Perrone, *1994, India,* FOLKLORE

A long time ago, a girl named Chandra lived in a small village in India. Chandra loves her job as the bather of the Rajah's elephants, and she loves math. But as she watches the elephants carry away almost all of the villagers' rice to pay rent to the Rajah, she becomes sad. One day, the elephants become sick, and only Chandra can cure them. The grateful Rajah promises her any treasure she wants. All she wants is two grains of rice on the first square of a chessboard, doubled each square until the last. She's an ingenious girl, and math lovers and phobics alike will delight in her victory and be amazed at the magnitude of her success.

The Red Comb, Fernando Picó, illustrated by Maria Antonia Ordóñez, *1991, Puerto Rico,* HISTORICAL FICTION

Pedro Calderón makes money for each runaway slave he catches, but not everyone in their Puerto Rican village agrees with his actions. Siña Rosa reminds people that their own grandparents were often escaped slaves, while next door, her young neighbor Vitita listens carefully to what she says. When Vitita discovers a runaway slave under her house, she and Rosa work together to save her, leaving her food and repeatedly outwitting a persistent Pedro Calderón. The story's serious message concerning slavery is leavened by Siña Rosa's often hilarious tricks on Pedro Calderón and by a happy and satisfying ending. The illustrations develop a similar contrast: bright tropical colors, lush surroundings, and the glow of young faces gain depth alongside the wild hair of the runaway slave and the strong and harshly etched face of Siña Rosa.

> *My aunt, who was an actress, would read to me and my three younger sisters from Grimm's Fairy Tales. I was six, yet I knew who I wanted to be . . . The Wicked Queen from Snow White.*
>
> *Rosalee, poet*

Rimonah of the Flashing Sword: A North African Tale, Eric A. Kimmel, illustrated by Omar Rayyan, *1995, Egypt,* FOLKLORE

This North African version of Snow White makes the Disney movie look positively vapid. The story line is similar: a wicked sorceress marries the king and plots his beautiful daughter's death. This time, the heroine is Rimonah, "with skin as dark as a pomegranate's peel." When she is abandoned in the desert, Rimonah finds her way not to a group of singing dwarfs, but into a den of thieves, where she is soon an accepted member of their group and becomes "the boldest of the band." After she is poisoned by the queen, placed in a glass coffin, and revived by a kiss, Rimonah awakens to help lead the attack on her nemesis, resolved to save her father and the kingdom.

Dramatic, highly stylized watercolor illustrations bring out a mythical feeling in Eric Kimmel's adaptation of the old folktale, which places more value on courage than on beauty.

Roses Sing on New Snow: A Delicious Tale, Paul Yee, illustrated by Harvey Chan, *1991, Canada,* FICTION

Maylin does all the cooking in her father's Chinatown restaurant, but in turn-of-the-century Canada, girls are not supposed to be cooks, so Maylin's father always claims his sons are his chefs. It is Maylin, however, who has the love of cooking and uses her skills to make the men newly arrived from China feel less homesick. When the governor of South China comes and asks all the restaurants to make their best dishes, Maylin creates a new dish, Roses Sing on New Snow. The governor loves it and wants to meet the cook—and that's where the real trouble begins. Richly detailed watercolors add to this story that teaches not only about equality, but about the differences between individuals and between worlds new and old.

Ruth Law Thrills a Nation, Don Brown, author and illustrator, *1993, United States,* BIOGRAPHY

Back in 1916, Ruth Law became the first person to try to fly from Chicago to New York in one day. It was going to be cold, so Ruth put on many layers of clothing—two woolen, two leather, plus the mandatory skirt. With her maps strapped to her leg, flying a mile above the ground, she traveled at one hundred miles an hour. The illustrations depict the reality of Ruth's challenge; sitting without any protection on what is basically a bicycle with wings, she flies far above tiny, tiny farms. Night comes and Ruth must stop before she reaches New York, but she set the American nonstop cross-country flying record. It was broken the next year—by another woman.

[Books] bring me hope.

Bailey, poet

Sachiko Means Happiness, Kimiko Sakai, illustrated by Tomie Arai, *1990, United States,* FICTION

Sachiko can remember the days when she rode on her grandmother's strong back and when they read stories sitting close together. Now Grandmother can't remember who Sachiko is, and it makes Sachiko frustrated and angry. One evening, when Grandmother insists she is five years old and must go home, Sachiko lets her out into the night and follows her. During this walk, Sachiko comes to understand what Alzheimer's disease means for her grandmother. In a powerful and touching ending, Sachiko accepts her grandmother's condition, and, speaking to her as if she were indeed a lost five-year-old, Sachiko invites her home.

The Samurai's Daughter, Robert D. San Souci, illustrated by Stephen T. Johnson, *1992, Japan,* FOLKLORE

Tokoyo, the only child of a widowed samurai, is the apple of her father's eye. He teaches her the virtues of courage, endurance, and discipline and instills in her an awareness of those less fortunate than herself. Tokoyo loves to dive deep into the ocean with other women, harvesting oysters and abalone. One day, her father tells her that the emperor, who is under a sorcerer's spell, has banished him to a faraway island. At first brokenhearted, Tokoyo resolves to either rescue her father or join him in exile. There are bandits for Tokoyo to contend with, a frightening, ghostly warrior ship that "washed over her like chill mist," and a demon sea serpent that she battles one-on-one. Stephen Johnson uses mood-altering pastels and sparseness of design to highlight the love between Tokoyo and her father, illuminate the risks she faces on her quest, and take the reader underwater with her on her numerous dives into the sea.

Saturday Sancocho, Leyla Torres, author and illustrator, *1995, South America,* FICTION

On Saturdays, Maria Lili and her grandparents always make chicken sancocho together. But today Papa Angelino tells her they have no money to buy the necessary ingredients; in fact, all they have is a dozen eggs. But Mama Ana has a plan, and putting the eggs in a basket, off to the market she and Maria Lili go. Down the hillside we can see the market, full of vegetables, people, and a dog or two roaming around. Mama Ana is soon bartering some eggs for plantains, then plantains for cassava, cassava for corn. At the stalls we learn each seller's name and a little about Mama Ana's skills at keeping everyone happy while getting the ingredients she needs. The market feels alive as cheerful watercolors capture the movement and motion of the people. By Saturday afternoon, at the regular time, Maria Lili, Papa Angelino, and clever Mama Ana are enjoying a hot bowl of delicious sancocho stew.

> *Yama's eyes grew wide as he stared at Savitri. "You did not ask for your husband's life, yet I cannot grant your wish without releasing him. Princess, your wit is as strong as your will."*
> *from* Savitri: A Tale of Ancient India *by Aaron Shepard*

Savitri: A Tale of Ancient India, Aaron Shepard, illustrated by Vera Rosenberry, *1992, India,* FOLKLORE

This well-loved Indian legend is taken from *The Mahabharata*, an epic written more than two thousand years ago. Savitri is beautiful and intelligent, yet no man approaches her for marriage. Her father tells her: "Weak men turn away from radiance like yours. Go out and find a man worthy of you." Savitri falls in love with the kind and virtuous Prince Satyavan, although a holy seer tells Savitri that the prince will be dead in one year. They are very happy together, but as their anniversary approaches, Savitri fasts and prays. On the anticipated day, Prince Satyavan dies, but because of her fasting and prayers, Savitri is able to see and follow Yama, the god of death, when he takes Prince Satyavan. Three times Yama tells her to turn back, yet because he admires Savitri's courage and devotion, each time he grants her a wish, and finally she outwits him. The graceful and elegant watercolors, lovely in their detail and soft colors, perfectly complement this rich story.

The Selkie Girl, Susan Cooper, illustrated by Warwick Hutton, *1986, Scotland,* FOLKLORE

"The islands rise green out of the sea, where the waves foam over the grey rocks, and strange things may happen there." There is an old legend from Scotland and Ireland of the selkie, or seal-people. Once a year, "they get the land-longing on them" and shed their sealskins to become human. In this telling of the legend, a young man named Donallan falls in love with a selkie and steals her skin so she will stay with him. They are happy together and have children, yet there is always something sad about Mairi. Eventually Mairi has the chance to return to the sea, and she does, leaving her children with the understanding that she loves them and will always watch over them. Gracefully written, *The Selkie Girl* teaches much about maternal love and each person's need to be true to oneself.

Seya's Song, Ron Hirschi, illustrated by Constance Bergum, *1992, United States,* FICTION

Seya's Song is a beautifully illustrated, lyrical look into a way of thinking and speaking. A girl takes a walk by a stream, remembering the S'Klallam words her grandmother, Seya, taught her. The narration follows the themes of seasons, growth, and a way of life: "When Grandmother and Grandfather were young, S'Klallam words were with us like the wind, the songs of birds, and the swirl of the tide. Our voices were the only human sound—gentle and kind, yet strong voices that were one with the seasons of salmon and cedar." *Seya's Song* is imbued with the feeling of loss and celebration, as the young girl carries on those traditions that are still a part of her life.

A Sled Dog for Moshi, Jeanne Bushey, illustrated by Germaine Ar-naktauyok, *1994, Canada,* FICTION

Moshi's dad raises sled dogs in their remote village near the Arctic Circle. Here people have dogs for pulling sleds or racing, not as house pets. When Jessica, Moshi's friend who has recently moved from the city, gets a dog for a pet, Moshi wants a dog like that, one that will do tricks and can stay in the house. One day the young girls get lost in a white-out, and Moshi proves to be very resourceful in keeping the girls safe and providing comfort for Jessica. But it is when her dad's favorite dog Nuna comes to their aid that Moshi learns the value of a sled dog. The traditional artwork by Inuit artist Germaine Arnaktauyok energizes this genial tale of how connected we all are—nature, animals, and people.

The Story of Ruby Bridges, Robert Coles, illustrated by George Ford, *1995, United States,* BIOGRAPHY

In 1960, six-year-old Ruby Bridges became one of four black girls to integrate the elementary schools in New Orleans. Ruby was sent alone to William Frantz Elementary School. Each day, protected by the National Guard, she faced a mob of angry parents; each day, she sat with her teacher in an empty classroom. She never stopped going to school. One day, after her teacher saw her stop in the crowd and say something to herself, she asked Ruby what she was doing; Ruby told her she was praying for the crowd. A true story of courage and faith, *The Story of Ruby Bridges* offers younger readers an introduction to the Civil Rights movement and an awe-inspiring role model.

> *The universe is made of stories, not of atoms.*
> *Muriel Rukeyser, writer*

The Story of Stagecoach Mary Fields, Robert H. Miller, illustrated by Cheryl Hanna, *1995, United States,* BIOGRAPHY

The Pony Express is the stuff of myth and legends, but most people don't know about Mary Fields, a cigar-smoking, gun-toting African-American woman who took on one of the toughest stagecoach mail service routes at the age of sixty. Mary Fields was born a slave in 1832 and lived on a plantation in Tennessee until the Civil War was ended. Later she went to St. Peter's Mission in Montana and became boss of the construction crew fixing up the mission. After a shoot-out with an employee who didn't like taking orders from a black woman, Mary took a job with the postal service, where she fought off bandits, wolves, and bad weather to haul mail for eight years. Her story can make your jaw drop, and the pencil-and-ink illustrations show a strong and brawny Mary, worthy of her own legend or two.

Sweet Clara and the Freedom Quilt, Deborah Hopkinson, illustrated by James Ransome, *1993, United States,* HISTORICAL FICTION

Sweet Clara is a slave, sent away from her mother before she is even twelve. Realizing that Clara is not strong enough to survive fieldwork, Aunt Rachel teaches Clara to sew and gets her a job as a seamstress in the Big House. In the kitchen of the Big House, Clara hears many things—about runaway slaves, an Underground Railroad, the need for a map. Clara realizes that a quilt can be like a map, and bit by bit she gathers information and sews it into a pattern no one has ever seen before. And when Clara runs away, she leaves the quilt behind for others to use: "Sometimes I wish I could sew a quilt that would spread over the whole land, and the people just follow the stitches to freedom, as easy as taking a Sunday walk." Glowing paintings by James Ransome enchance this suspenseful adventure story and important history lesson.

The Tangerine Tree, Regina Hanson, illustrated by Harvey Stevenson, *1995, Jamaica,* FICTION

Because there is no work in Jamaica, Ida's papa has to go to a job in New York. Before he leaves, Papa gives Ida a book and tells her that when she can read it, he will be home again. In the meantime, her job is to help the tangerine tree grow the best fruit. When Papa goes, she gives him a bottle of tangerine juice, some of Mistress Sun to take with him to cold New York. And after he is gone, she sits herself down in Mama's safe lap, because "I goin' to know dis book fast. Den I will read all de books Teacher have at school. And den I will write to Papa and tell him it's time to come home." Rough pastel drawings seem ready to burst with oranges and yellows, deep purples and blues, the pink of a little girl's dress, and the love of a father and daughter as they lean foreheads together to say good-bye.

> *Sasifi stretched her body taller and took big steps to keep up with Mama. Of course she was big enough to help!*
>
> *from* Tap-Tap *by Karen Lynn Williams*

Tap-Tap, Karen Lynn Williams, illustrated by Catherine Stock, *1994, Haiti,* FICTION

Finally Sasifi is eight years old and can help her mother take their produce to sell at the local market. It's a long walk, and Sasifi wishes more than once that they had the money to take one of the brightly painted tap-taps that pass them on the road, filled with passengers. At the market, Sasifi is a responsible helper, and her mother gives her money of her own at the end of the day, to choose whatever she wants to buy. You got it—and so will many young readers—Sasifi wants to ride a tap-tap home. Her journey and the lessons she learns from it are simple and reassuring ones, made cheerful and warm by the watercolor illustrations. The story is a wonderful mix; while the concept of taking on responsibility and enjoying it is a universal one, the setting—full of atmosphere, bright color, and small local details—places readers directly in Sasifi's Haitian village.

Tar Beach, Faith Ringold, author and illustrator, *1991, United States,* FANTASY

"Anyone can fly. All you need is somewhere to go that you can't get to any other way. The next thing you know, you're flying among the stars." Cassie Lou Lightfoot, eight years old in 1939, loves sleeping on Tar Beach, the roof of their apartment building. Looking out to the George Washington Bridge, where her Daddy once worked, she feels as if she owns everything. Reality, though, is harder. Daddy can't always get work, and people call him Colored, or Half-Breed. In her dreams, Cassie's father is rich, her mother is happy, and they have ice cream for dessert every night. Faith Ringold brings these dreams alive, as we follow Cassie on her nighttime flights, arms spread wide to hold the whole sky.

Tatterhood and the Hobgoblins, Lauren Mills, author and illustrator, *1993, Norway,* FOLKLORE

Tatterhood is a princess, "wild and strange," who cavorts about the palace grounds in a ragged cloak, riding a donkey and carrying a wooden spoon. While Tatterhood is a challenge to her mother, she is a loving friend to her "tame and beautiful" twin sister, and it is brave and intrepid Tatterhood who, at the age of twelve, saves her sister from the hobgoblins. Later, when the two sisters meet their potential spouses, Tatterhood wisely waits until her prince has appreciated her for her unusual self before she discards her tattered cloak and tangled hair and becomes a magnificent and self-assured princess. Tatterhood glows in all her curly-haired wildness in the midst of illustrations filled with the muted colors and wicked goblins reminiscent of traditional European folktales.

> *I recall reading with such intensity that my mother forbade me to go to the 82nd Street library because I was so inflamed with fairy stories I couldn't sleep.*
>
> Richard Stern, *writer*

This Time, Tempe Wick?, Patricia Lee Gauch, illustrated by Margot Tomes, *1974, United States,* BIOGRAPHICAL FICTION

Patricia Gauch has commented, "I guess you can say I'm after truth, but the kind that sketches a human in good, hefty proportions." Tempe Wick was a real young woman who lived during the Revolutionary War years. Patricia Gauch presents her as a Paul Bunyan-like character, large in stature and able to beat the boys at wrestling. When ten thousand soldiers spend two winters (1780 and 1781) near her house, she doesn't mind the inconvenience, even though her mother is sick and her father has died, and the soldiers eat much of their food. But when the soldiers mutiny and several threaten to steal her horse, Tempe gets mad. How she saves her horse, gets medicine for her mother, and outwits the soldiers is worth the price of admission.

Three Days on a River in a Red Canoe, Vera B. Williams, author and illustrator, *1981, United States,* FICTION

Before the narrator was born, her mother and Aunt Rosie used to take canoe trips all the time. Now the narrator has found a red canoe for sale, and along with cousin Sam they are all going canoeing. Through the young narrator's journal, complete with whimsical, colored-pencil drawings, we go with them as they buy supplies, plan a route, set out in the mist, portage around a waterfall, make fruit stew and dumplings (we even get a recipe), discover rainbows, and almost lose their canoe in a nighttime hurricane—all the ups and downs of a magnificent camping trip. You may be inspired to take your own trip, now that you know what it's like.

Three Strong Women: A Tall Tale from Japan, Claus Stamm, illustrated by Jean Tseng and Mou-sien Tseng, *1962, Japan,* FOLKLORE

Forever-Mountain believes he is the strongest person in Japan. While walking to the capital city to wrestle for the Emperor, he sneaks up on Maru-me to tickle her. Before he knows what has happened, Maru-me has caught him and won't let him go. Not only is he embarrassed, his hand is getting sore. Maru-me takes him home to teach him how to be a really strong person so he won't get hurt while wrestling at the capital. Maru-me and her mother are obviously too powerful for Forever-Mountain to practice with, but grandmother probably can't injure him. Three months later, when Forever-Mountain wins the prize at the capital, it's clear he has learned that strength is not only physical. With its gleeful illustrations, *Three Strong Women* humorously exaggerates everyone's strengths and leaves us with a happy ending.

Too Many Tamales, Gary Soto, illustrated by Ed Martinez, *1993, United States,* FICTION

It's Christmas Eve and Marie is having a great time helping her parents make tamales. While kneading the masa dough, Marie slips on her Mom's diamond ring, the ring that sparkles like Christmas lights. When the relatives arrive, Marie and her cousins run upstairs to play. Then Marie remembers the ring; she is sure that it must be in one of the cooked tamales. Down to the kitchen go Marie and her three cousins, where they begin to eat the tamales. They eat, and they eat some more, each of them waiting to bite into something hard. They never find the ring, and a tearful Marie goes to tell her mother. Not to fear, a happy ending is had by all, and the entire family ends up in the kitchen, making another batch of tamales. Ed Martinez's luscious illustrations capture a happy and sad Marie, cousins with big eyes and big bellies, and the warmth of the holiday season.

> *Books are keys to wisdom's treasure; / Books are gates to lands of pleasure; / Books are paths that upward lead; / Books are friends. Come, let us read.*
>
> Emilie Poulsson, poet

Treasure Nap, Juanita Havill, illustrated by Elivia Savadier, *1992, United States and Mexico,* FICTION

Alicia and her Mama agree that it's too hot to take a nap. So they spread a big blue sheet out on the floor and Mama tells Alicia the story she loves to hear. Long ago a little girl named Rita lived in Mexico. She went to her grandfather's village in the mountains with her Mama and baby brother. Grandfather made birdcages and played the pito so the birds would come near. Rita loved her grandfather and was sad when it was time to leave, but Grandfather gave Rita a birdcage, pito, and serape to take with her when her family moved to the United States. After the story, Alicia falls asleep, and when she wakes up she opens an old trunk. Inside are the gifts Grandfather gave to Rita, for Rita is Alicia's great-grandmother. Brightly colored illustrations capture both Rita's and Alicia's joy in the treasures that have passed through generations.

Trouble with Trolls, Jan Brett, author and illustrator, *1992, Europe,* FANTASY

"My name is Treva, and I have had trouble with trolls," says the young blond-haired girl who grins at you from the first page. Thus begins a magical story of quick-thinking Treva, who outwits the trolls eager to steal her dog. As each troll confronts Treva, she convinces him that something else—her mittens, shoes, hat—is far more valuable. By the end, she has almost nothing left, but get it all back she does, without losing her dog. The intricate and fantastical illustrations depict an energetic, happy girl, and an entire troll world that lies below, and sometimes around, the "real" world that Treva inhabits.

The Two of Them, Aliki, author and illustrator, *1979, United States,* FICTION

The Two of Them is a tender story of a grandfather who loves his granddaughter from the day she is born. He makes things for her, sings her songs, plays in the garden, tells her stories—some of them from long ago, some about his love for her. The seasons change, the years pass, and Grandfather becomes ill. His granddaughter sings him songs, takes him to the garden, tells him stories that he told her, and stories about her love for him. Although she knows he will die, when it happens, "she was not ready and she hurt inside and out." She watches the changes in the garden, thinks about the seasons, and remembers her grandfather. The soft watercolors of the granddaughter and grandfather illuminate their love and allow for her sad feelings as she sits in a spring garden.

Vasalisa and Her Magic Doll, Rita Grauer, author and illustrator, *1994, Russia,* FOLKLORE

When Vasalisa's mother dies, she leaves her house to Vasalisa's older sister, Svetlana, on the condition that she take care of Vasalisa. To Vasalisa, she leaves a small, magic doll. While Svetlana has good intentions, soon her jealousy over Vasalisa's beauty causes her to send Vasalisa out into the night, in search of fire from the dreaded Baba Yaga. Taking her doll, Vasalisa sets out and encounters many difficulties, each overcome as she follows the doll's advice: "Do what lies before you, and all will be well." Rita Grauer's adaptation of the Vasalisa story places a comforting emphasis on the courage of young girls and on the bonds between mothers, daughters, and sisters; the gentleness of the chalk-and-pencil illustrations softens the often scary Baba Yaga story.

Very Last First Time, Jan Andrews, illustrated by Ian Wallace, *1985, Canada,* FICTION

In the wintertime on Ungava Bay in northern Quebec, people break through ice shells that form offshore when the tide is out, and descend to the ocean floor to harvest mussels. *Very Last First Time* is the story of the first time that Eva, a young Inuit girl, goes alone below the ice to collect mussels. She sings while she works by candlelight in this fascinating world, and her voice echoes off the sea floor; soon her pan is full. Then she goes exploring and finds a rock pool with shrimp and sea anemones, and a shiny, slick seaweed bed, all illustrated in deeply textured watercolors full of greens, purples, and blues. When Eva's candle goes out, plunging her into total darkness, her fright is real. But she finds her way back, and dances in the moonlight shining through the hole in the ice. Safe above the seabed, Eva realizes that there is only one first time for everything.

> *Certain books come to meet one, as do people.*
> *Elizabeth Bowen, writer*

The Wednesday Surprise, Eve Bunting, illustrated by Donald Carrick, *1989, United States,* FICTION

The Wednesday Surprise radiates love across generations, and reminds us what a privilege it is to be able to read. On Wednesday nights, Mom works, Anna's brother goes to basketball practice, and Grandma comes to stay with Anna. Every week she brings a cloth bag loaded down with books, and Anna and Grandma go to work on their surprise for Anna's father's birthday. They read for an hour, stop for ice cream, read some more. Grandma looks at Anna and exclaims: "Only seven years old and smart as paint already!" On Dad's birthday, Grandma comes to his party with a bag of books. But when the time comes for the surprise, we are surprised as well, for it is Grandma, not Anna, who has been learning how to read.

What Mary Jo Shared, Janice May Udry, illustrated by Elizabeth Sayles, *1966, United States,* FICTION

Mary Jo really wants to share something at school, but she is too shy. Besides, every time she thinks of something, it turns out someone else had the same idea, only better. She brings one grasshopper; Jimmy brought six. She brings her new umbrella, but it seems everyone else has one, too. Every day her father asks her if she shared something, and she has to say no. Finally, Mary Jo thinks of something no one else has. We won't spoil what it is, but it's wonderful, as is the grin on Mary Jo's face at the book's end.

> *It had been startling and disappointing to me to find out that story books had been written by people, that books were not natural wonders, coming up of themselves like grass.*
>
> *Eudora Welty, writer*

The Widow's Broom, Chris Van Allsburg, author and illustrator, *1992, United States,* FANTASY

"Witches' brooms don't last forever. They grow old, and even the best of them, one day, lose the power of flight." The Widow Shaw is surprised to find an injured witch in her garden, but being a kindly person, she brings the witch into her cottage and puts her to bed to rest. By morning the witch is gone, but the broom isn't. Soon the broom is sweeping Widow Shaw's floors, constantly. She teaches this energetic broom how to chop wood, carry water, feed the chickens—why, it can even pick out simple piano tunes! The broom makes Widow Shaw's life so much easier, but the neighbors think that it is wicked and dangerous. Chris Van Allsburg, author of *The Polar Express* and *Jumanji*, once again enhances his story with spectacular pencil drawings that bring suspense and humor to this fine tale of fear and kindness, and leave us, in the end, with a happy widow and broom.

The Woman Who Flummoxed the Fairies, Heather Forest, illustrated by Susan Gaber, *1990, Scotland,* FOLKLORE

The bakerwoman makes the most wonderful cakes in the world, and the fairies are furious. You see, people eat every last crumb of the bakerwoman's cakes, and there is none left for the fairies. So the fairies capture the bakerwoman. She knows if the fairies ever taste her baking, they will never let her go. One by one, she requests ingredients, and then her dog, her baby—without them she cannot cook. The dog howls, the baby throws oatmeal, and the poor fairies—who hate commotion—finally agree to let the bakerwoman go home. Susan Gaber's illustrations whirl about with the magic of the fairies and the chaos orchestrated by the strong, caring, clever bakerwoman.

You're My Nikki, Phyllis Rose Eisenberg, illustrated by Jill Kastner, *1986, United States,* FICTION

Nikki's mother is going back to work, and Nikki is worried that her mother won't remember her while she is away. So Nikki follows her mother about the house, reminding her of all of Nikki's favorite things. Mom is reassuring, telling Nikki how much she loves her, how she could never forget her. Still, when Mom is done with her first day of work, she is absent-minded and seems to have forgotten things that Nikki thinks are essential. A reassuring bedtime talk makes all things right, and teaches Nikki a lesson about empathy as well. A loving book, *You're My Nikki* is especially good for children who are having problems sharing their parents with the outside world.

> *When I began to read the nursery rhymes for myself, and later, to read other verses and ballads, I knew I had discovered the most important things, to me, that could ever be.*
>
> Dylan Thomas, poet

CHAPTER BOOKS
AGES 6–11

These selections are for independent readers, although many can be read aloud to younger children. The books use relatively large type and fairly simple vocabulary; many have illustrations. Content ranges from carefree and reassuring stories to explorations of more challenging issues. Enjoy listening to a new reader as she tells you all about the book she has just read.

Now that you're an independent reader, you can choose your own books, and read your favorites over and over if you want. These books have fewer pictures; like a hand holding yours as you cross the street, you don't really need them, but sometimes you like the feeling anyway. What's important now is the words, and the exhilaration of reading by yourself.

Some books draw you in so you almost become the characters. You can feel the slime when the oops-it-wasn't-boiled egg slides down Ramona's hair, and listen as Laura's father plays his fiddle by the fire. When Eugenie Clark swims with the sharks, you're in the water, too. As you get older and become ready, books provide you with a safe place to contemplate difficult or confusing issues. At a time in your life when you are beginning to figure out who you are and where you fit in, books take you inside another person, looking out.

The Adventures of Mabel, Harry Thurston Peck, illustrated by Harry Rountree, *1986, United States,* FANTASY, *223 pages*

When five-year-old Mabel rescues the King of the Lizards, she receives a surprising gift: a special tune she can whistle that enables her to talk with animals. The whistle saves her from the jaws of a wolf, tames a bad-tempered horse, and enables her to make friends with the gray rat under the water pump. But that is not all. Mabel meets brownies and a giant, helps her horse identify robbers, gives herself a birthday party and invites only animals, and rescues a young boy. As her grandmother looks on in mild surprise, intrepid little Mabel careers about the countryside on her steed Rex, making friends and generally having the time of her life. Part fantasy, part nostalgia journey to a simpler time, *The Adventures of Mabel* makes a great early reader or read-aloud for younger children. Facsimile versions preserve the full-color illustrations that were created for the original 1896 edition.

> *"Hold out your hands," [Sequoyah] told her. Light filled Ahyoka's hands and flashed from her bracelet. "See how the sunshine dances. How can we ever draw words to say that?"*
>
> *from* Ahyoka and the Talking Leaves
> *by Connie and Peter Roop*

Ahyoka and the Talking Leaves: The Story of the Cherokee Alphabet, Connie and Peter Roop, illustrated by Yoshi Miyake, *1992, United States,* BIOGRAPHICAL FICTION, *58 pages*

Few people know that sequoia trees were named in honor of Sequoyah, the creator of the first Cherokee alphabet. Certain that the white man's ability to read gave him a distinct advantage, Sequoyah gave up his work as a silversmith, and with the help and encouragement of his daughter, Ahyoka, spent twelve years developing an alphabet. Many Cherokees, including his wife, were scared and angered by his work, but he never stopped. Written languages are almost always developed over long periods of time and through the help of many people. Sequoyah and Ahyoka did what no one had ever done before: create a written language from a spoken one by themselves. This short, accessible book, written from Ahyoka's perspective, reminds us of the magic and power of reading and writing.

Alice's Adventures in Wonderland, Lewis Carroll, illustrated by John Tenniel, *1865, England,* FANTASY, *191 pages*

Alice's Adventures in Wonderland is a story that sets the imagination soaring. Children and adults alike will delight in young Alice's finding herself in a world inhabited by a Cheshire cat that appears and disappears at will, a fretful white rabbit who is constantly running late, and the always angry Queen of Hearts, whose command "Off with their heads!" is never carried through. Alice tries to make sense of the nonsensical world she lands in after falling through a rabbit's hole, but she soon realizes that she's in a place where she doesn't know the rules. Lewis Carroll makes his readers laugh with continual puns and a madcap pace; John Tenniel's illustrations are a visual feast. *Alice's Adventures in Wonderland* is a book to read aloud with children to see their eyes sparkle; a child reading it alone can escape into the never-never land of words.

All for the Better: A Story of El Barrio, Nicholasa Mohr, illustrated by Rudy Gutierrez, *1993, United States,* BIOGRAPHY, *56 pages*

In 1933, Evelina Lopez's mother found herself with three children and no money, so Evelina, the oldest at age eleven, was sent from Puerto Rico to live with relatives in New York City. Evelina didn't want to go; she hardly remembered her aunt and didn't know her uncle. Capturing Evelina's steadfast and generous spirit, Nicholasa Mohr explores Evelina's life in a new homeland. Within days of her arrival, she is attending school and learning English. Though she longs for her family and is confused by the ridicule of her classmates, she studies hard and does well. A firm believer in the good in people, she finds ways to help those in need. In Spanish Harlem in those days there were many people who couldn't find work, yet were too proud to accept government aid; Evelina helped people fill out the forms and made the journey across town to pick up their food. When Evelina grew up, she fought for school reform and led a nonviolent protest against the closure of public libraries in her area. This insightful book focuses on Evelina's life as a child, and demonstrates the impact one person can have.

All-of-a-Kind Family, Sydney Taylor, illustrated by Helen John, *1951, United States,* FICTION, *189 pages*

All-of-a-Kind Family transports readers to turn-of-the-century New York City and into the lives of a large and loving family. The five "stair-step" daughters, all two years apart, range in age from four to twelve and share one bedroom. Papa works hard in his second-hand shop, but there are few luxuries in their lives. They have riches through their love of books, each other, friends, and their Jewish religion. Throughout the book we celebrate the Sabbath, Passover, Purim, and Sukkot. The many visits to the library, the markets, and Papa's shop reveal the girls' personalities as their day-to-day lives unfold with their ups and downs and generally happy resolutions. This warm and generous story is the first in a series.

> *No entertainment is so cheap as reading, nor any pleasure as lasting.*
>
> Mary Wortley Montagu, essayist and poet

Anastasia Krupnik, Lois Lowry, illustrated by Diane de Groat, *1979, United States,* FICTION, *113 pages*

Anastasia writes her important thoughts in her private green notebook: her favorite words, the beginnings of poems, lists of things she loves and hates. At ten years old she is both confident and confused. She wants to be in charge of her life, but so many aspects of it are out of her control—the wart on her left thumb, her grandmother's forgetful mind, the baby growing in her mother's stomach.

Lois Lowry humorously depicts Anastasia's emotional growth, particularly through the changes on her love and hate lists. To her parents, she and her observations of life are a constant surprise; to her readers, she is a marvel, and they may want to follow caring, precocious Anastasia through other titles of this series.

The Baby Grand, the Moon in July, & Me, Joyce Annette Barnes, *1994, United States,* FICTION, *134 pages*

Joyce Barnes sets her novel in the five days between Wednesday, July 16, 1969, when *Apollo 11* lifted off, and Sunday, July 20, when the first man walked on the moon. Almost-eleven-year-old Annie Armstrong is completely captivated by the events that are occurring on her television screen. She walks about spouting rocket speed figures and lunar facts and talks of her ambition to be an astronaut. Her brother Matty, nine years older, wants to play jazz, although his father is sure he will amount to nothing. When Matty has a baby grand piano (bought on credit) delivered to their home, it sets off a terrific conflict and in the end, Matty leaves. Annie wants peace in her family, but her plan to regain it requires her to overcome some of her own fears and myths. Pulling the threads of the novel together, Joyce Barnes makes us realize that in working to reunite her father and brother, Annie learns the courage and resolve she will need to follow her own dream of becoming an astronaut.

Baby Island, Carol Ryrie Brink, illustrated by Helen Sewell, *1937, Scotland,* FICTION, *160 pages*

Readers may be more familiar with Carol Brink's *Caddie Woodlawn*, but *Baby Island* deserves its own special mention. As it begins, twelve-year-old Mary and her younger sister Jean are traveling alone on an ocean liner to Australia to meet their father. When the ship starts to sink, Mary immediately sets out to save all the babies. Mary, Jean, a pair of two-year-old twins, and two babies are set adrift in a lifeboat. Sound terrifying? Mary and Jean are thrilled—finally, they have the babies to themselves. Their pluck and solid common sense make this an amazingly good-natured and fun book, sure to bring smiles to future female Robinson Crusoes and maternal types alike.

Barbara McClintock: Alone in Her Field, Deborah Heiligman, illustrated by Janet Hamlin, *1994, United States,* BIOGRAPHY, *60 pages*

When Barbara McClintock was born in 1902, her parents named her Eleanor, but a few months later they changed it. "Eleanor" seemed too soft for this little girl, and she became Barbara. As a child, Barbara asked her mother to make her bloomers instead of dresses; when she went to college, she chopped off her hair and wanted to study genetics. Because she was a woman, she wasn't allowed in the genetics department, so she enrolled in cytology (the study of cells) and then spent her career researching how the chromosomes of corn plants pass on genetic information. The scientific community thought her ideas were crazy, but she didn't care. Finally, three decades after her initial discoveries, her work was recognized and she was awarded the Nobel Prize.

Betsy-Tacy, Maud Hart Lovelace, illustrated by Lois Lenski, *1940, United States,* FICTION, *113 pages*

Betsy-Tacy is the first in a series of charming books about two five-year-old friends, Betsy Ray and Tacy Kelly, set back in a time when father drove a horse and carriage to work and little girls could explore about the countryside without supervision. Fanciful and nostalgic, *Betsy-Tacy* also deals with some serious issues—the death of an infant sibling, the birth of a baby and some corresponding sibling jealousy, and misunderstandings between friends. Some may find the book too sweet, but for others, *Betsy-Tacy* will be a safe haven of friendship and warmth, where technology has not yet arrived and life is a little slower than most of us are used to.

Binya's Blue Umbrella, Ruskin Bond, illustrated by Vera Rosenberry, *1995, India,* FICTION, *68 pages*

Although she sometimes lollygags behind and her mother has to ask her more than once to get her chores done, ten-year-old Binya is a happy girl with a quick smile. While tending her cows one day,

Binya comes upon some picnickers from the city. One of the women eyes Binya's unique tiger claw necklace and wants it. Binya won't sell it; instead she trades her necklace for the woman's blue silk umbrella. The people in her village, who don't have the luxury of owning something just for its beauty, have never seen such an umbrella. But Binya knows the umbrella's purpose is its beauty. Ram Bharosa, who owns the local tea shop, wants to own the umbrella, but Binya refuses to sell, and when Ram Bharosa uses an underhanded move to try to get what he wants, his action costs him the villagers' respect. In the end, Binya, wise beyond her years, shows the meaning of friendship to Ram Bharosa and the villagers.

> *As you read a book word by word and page by page, you partici-*
> *pate in its creation. . . . And, as you read and re-read, the book*
> *of course participates in the creation of you, your thoughts and*
> *feelings, the size and temper of your soul.*
>
> Ursula K. Le Guin, *writer*

The Canada Geese Quilt, Natalie Kinsey-Warnock, illustrated by Leslie W. Bowman, *1989, United States,* FICTION, *60 pages*

In the springtime, when the Canada geese fly north, Ariel's mother announces she is going to have another baby. After ten years of being an only child, Ariel is unprepared for the news. But Grandma lets her know about the special love of being a sister, then suggests they make a gift together for the baby—Grandma will quilt a picture that Ariel draws. When Grandma has a stroke, Ariel feels alone, frightened by this woman who hardly walks and slurs her words. After hearing her mother cry that Grandma has given up hope, Ariel realizes that if she were sick, Grandma would do anything to help her get well. Drawing on her powerful love for Grandma, Ariel begins to share memories with her, brings her an autumn leaf, and strolls with her on the farm, slowly coming to understand that although Grandma isn't the same on the outside, her heart and love haven't changed.

Cherokee Summer, Diane Hoyt-Goldsmith, photographs by Lawrence Migdale, *1993, United States,* NONFICTION, *32 pages*

The readers of *Cherokee Summer* get to spend it with ten-year-old Bridget, a Cherokee girl who lives in Okay, a small Oklahoma town. With pride, Bridget tells us some of her people's history, from 1838—when her ancestors were forced to walk from the Appalachian Mountains to the Oklahoma Territory—to her closing chapter of a Summer Stomp Dance, where she explains that dancing gives people "peace of mind." As Bridget explains how the Cherokee Nation governs itself, we visit Tahlequah, Oklahoma, a town that is at the heart of Cherokee political and social life. She introduces us to her family and Cherokee traditions, from quilting and basketmaking to arrowheads and blow guns. In a wonderful chapter on the Cherokee language, complete with a Cherokee syllabary, Bridget explains how using storytelling, legends, and a computer at the library helped her to learn the language. The color photographs on every page invite browsing, and the short chapters make for entertaining and informative reading.

Circle of Gold, Candy Dawson Boyd, *1984, United States,* FICTION, *124 pages*

Since Mattie's father died, nothing is the same. Her mother is always sad and constantly tired from working two jobs—and it's obvious to Mattie that her brother is Mother's favorite. Mattie believes if she can just earn the money to buy her mother a beautiful gold and pearl pin for Mother's Day, everything will be fine. But Mattie's baby-sitting job just ended, and while an essay contest offers a big prize, Mattie doubts her writing skills. In addition, Angel Higgley has accused Mattie of stealing her bracelet. As Mattie finds her way through each of her problems, she learns a lot about love, honesty, and miracles.

Clever Gretchen and Other Forgotten Folktales, Alison Lurie, illustrated by Margaret Tomes, *1980, Europe,* FOLKLORE, *113 pages*

Most of the heroines in Alison Lurie's collection use their prodigious brain power and imagination to accomplish their goals, often in remarkably witty ways: Clever Gretchen saves her husband from the Evil One; Manka proves she is wiser than her husband the judge; Mizilca—who dresses as a man to take her father's place as a soldier—keeps one step ahead of the Sultan's efforts to discover her gender; the Mastermaid helps her prince meet the demands of the giant; and Molly Whuppie outwits a giant not once but three times. Focusing largely on European folktales, the author also includes a clever variation of Sleeping Beauty (a Spanish folktale called "The Sleeping Prince") and the courageous tale of the girl who rescued Tom Lin from the fairies. These short stories are fun to read aloud; generally upbeat and rarely scary, they make good bedtime fare for a wide range of ages.

> *When I was in fifth grade I was known as the official groaner. Our teacher read us books, but they were always about boys. When I asked her about books with girls, she told me that all those books were boring.*
>
> *Colleen Sullivan, fisheries biologist*

Coast to Coast with Alice, Patricia Rusch Hyatt, *1991, United States,* HISTORICAL FICTION, *70 pages*

Patricia Hyatt has taken facts found in history books, newspapers, and memoirs, drawn on her imagination, and written a fascinating story of the first women to drive an automobile across the United States. The book is presented as the diary of fifteen-year-old Minna Jahns, who is accompanying twenty-one-year-old Alice Ramsey on this historic trip in 1909. Minna and Alice are strong-willed, independent young women, but Minna's parents insist that Alice's two sisters-in-law go along as chaperones. Much of the area they travel through has neither road maps nor roads. It's an adventure that has them getting stuck in the mud, eating dust, being attacked by bedbugs, and fixing flat tires and broken axles. They meet people who cheer them on and others who are certain women can't accomplish such a feat. Along with automotive history, Minna's frank observations of people and places, and numerous photographs, there is a building sense of excitement as the four women drive from New York to San Francisco on this road trip extraordinaire.

The Courage of Sarah Noble, Alice Dalgliesh, illustrated by Leonard Weisgard, *1954, United States,* BIOGRAPHICAL FICTION, *54 pages*

The Courage of Sarah Noble is based on the true story of an eight-year-old girl who accompanied her father into the wilderness of Connecticut in 1707 to build a house for their family. Sarah has full need of her courage as she travels and sleeps outside, then lives in a cave while her father builds the house. Always, she is afraid of Indians—at least until she meets the Indian children who live nearby. When Sarah's father returns to fetch the rest of the family, he leaves her with an Indian family, where she lives safely and happily until his return. Sarah is a brave and open-minded little girl, and her story is easily accessible for young readers.

> *Starch. The word had an odd sound to it, like a galaxy that was pulling apart, everything starching out faster and faster . . . scattering stardust in a fine, white spray over a pitch-black sky, the stars spreading away from one another. Star plus stretch equals starch, she told herself.*
>
> *from* Crossing the Starlight Bridge *by Alice Mead*

Crossing the Starlight Bridge, Alice Mead, *1994, United States,* FICTION, *120 pages*

Rayanne is a bit of a loner, but like all of us, she needs love. On her ninth birthday, her father gives her a big box of crayons and tells her he is leaving home for a while; she throws the crayons against the wall as he drives away. Eventually Ray and her mom leave the security of Two Rivers Island and the only home she has known to move onto the mainland with Ray's gram. Ray doesn't want any more changes and she worries: Will she be the only Wabanaki at her school? Will she ever stop being frightened by the traffic and noise of a city? When will her dad be back? Ray's keen observations of people and places help her adjust; her longings for island life are eased by Gram's humor and her stories that recall the pleasure of nature and animals. Slowly Ray's heart begins to heal, enabling her to move beyond her anger when her dad returns.

Daughter of the Mountains, Louise Rankin, illustrated by Kurt Wiese, *1948, Tibet and India,* FICTION, *191 pages*

Momo and her family live in a Tibetan village on the Khyber Pass, and many traders stop at her family's teahouse on their way through the Himalayan Mountains to India. When a trader gives Momo a Lhasa terrier, a dog she longed for, her heart is full. When another trader steals her dog to sell in Calcutta, her heart is broken. Momo knows her dog, Pempa, is meant to bring her family adventure and good fortune, so she must get Pempa back. Ten-year-old Momo needs her courage, religious faith, luck, and determination to see her through this dangerous journey. It is full of encounters, good and bad. The variety of terrain and people Momo confronts offers an amazing view of the land, lifestyles, and religions of this area just before the end of British rule. Generous Momo is a child guided by "the protection of the gods," and although she is seeking only her dog's return, this journey will affect her and many others long after it is finished.

Falcon's Egg, Luli Gray, *1995, United States,* FANTASY, *133 pages*

When Falcon finds the egg in Central Park, she is sure it is something unusual. It's fairly big, quite red, and so hot she has to wrap both her socks around it in order to carry it home. She knows she'll have to hide it; once, when she found a robin's egg, Missy, her mother, made her take it back, and now that Falcon's father has left and Missy has a "deadline," Falcon doesn't think Missy would understand about keeping a big, red, hot egg. Falcon enlists the help of her upstairs neighbor, her great-great-aunt Emily (who has a little magic in her own background), and Aunt Emily's ornithologist friend. By the time the egg hatches into a tiny dragon, even Falcon's little brother Toody is involved. As with all things wild, the dragon must eventually be set free, and as Falcon goes through the process of watching and caring for her dragon, she learns a lot about magic and life.

> *I hated childhood and spent it sitting behind a book waiting for adulthood to arrive.*
>
> Anne Tyler, *writer*

A Gift for Mama, Esther Hautzig, illustrated by Donna Diamond, *1981, Poland,* FICTION, *56 pages*
    "Sara was sick and tired of making presents. And Mother's Day was coming." All over the house, Sara's past presents are on display, and Mama has stated clearly that she doesn't believe in children buying presents. Fully aware of her mother's feelings, Sara still wants to buy her mother a pair of beautiful black satin slippers trimmed with blue leather. She knows they will make her mother look like a movie star. But the slippers cost nine zlotys, and Sara has none. The story of how she earns the money and her mother's approval is lovingly told, reminding children that effort and imagination are two of the most important elements in a gift. The monoprint illustrations reinforce the story's themes, for monoprints are created by painting on glass and then transferring a single, unique impression to paper. In shades of black, gray, and white, they show a close-knit family and their hometown of Vilna, Poland, more than fifty years ago.

The Gift-Giver, Joyce Hansen, *1980, United States,* FICTION, *118 pages*
    Ten-year-old Doris lives on 163rd Street in the Bronx. She wants to be like the rest of her friends and hang around the playground after school, but her mother says it's not safe and she wants Doris at home. Frustrated, Doris keeps rebelling, and it seems she'll be under punishment forever. Then slight, big-eyed Amir moves onto her block. He doesn't seem to care what others think; he doesn't participate in games, yet soon he is having an effect upon everyone.

Sherman stops bullying, Yellow Bird starts studying, and Doris learns how to do what she thinks is right in this story about friendship, growing up, and believing in yourself.

A Girl Called Bob and a Horse Called Yoki (also titled ***Taking Care of Yoki***), Barbara Campbell, *1982, United States,* FICTION, *167 pages*
Bob—or Barbara Ann, if you must—has two problems, made worse by her third problem, which is that her father is away fighting in World War II and isn't there for Bob to talk with. Her father might understand why Bob just can't let Mr. Strausberger's old milk delivery horse go to the glue factory. And he might be able to help her decide if she's ready to be baptized. For example, if she gets baptized, will she always have to do the right thing—and how do you know what the right thing is? More specifically, can a horse stealer be baptized? Although the questions are weighty, the book is not. It is enlivened by Bob's energetic personality, the bustling St. Louis setting, the humorous eccentricities of the landlady, the complicated relationship between Bob and her grandmother, and the wonderful dynamic that develops between Bob and her schoolmate Chuckie, once her nemesis, now her accomplice.

The Girl-Son, Anne E. Neuberger, *1995, Korea,* BIOGRAPHICAL FICTION, *119 pages*
This inspirational, fictionalized biography tells the story of Induk Pahk, born in 1894 to a scholarly father and an illiterate mother. When Induk is six, cholera takes her father's life, leaving Induk's mother with difficult choices. She can follow accepted practice and become the property of her husband's family, or she can try to provide for herself and daughter. She moves to another village, weaves cloth to sell, and—dressing her daughter as a boy because she knows of no school that accepts girls—tells Induk she is her "girl-son." When Induk's mother finds out about a Methodist mission school for girls, she leaves eight-year-old Induk at the school with a bag of rice and a cooker, and goes on the road as a peddler. Four years later, an independent Induk graduates. With faith, luck, and determination, Induk eventually becomes a teacher in Korea's first college for

women. Told through Induk's voice, *The Girl-Son* weaves a personal, cultural, and political history of Korea.

> *Grace loved military life. "I didn't even have to bother to decide what I was going to wear in the morning," she said. "I didn't have to figure out what I was going to cook for dinner. . . . I had a perfectly heavenly time."*
>
> *from* Grace Hopper: Programming Pioneer
> *by Nancy Whitelaw*

Grace Hopper: Programming Pioneer, Nancy Whitelaw, illustrated by Janet Hamlin, *1995, United States,* BIOGRAPHY, *60 pages*

The first woman to receive the National Medal of Technology, an admiral in the U.S. Navy, and the "grandmother" of the first symbolic language for computers, Grace Hopper started her career with computers when she joined the WAVES, the Navy's women's corps. The first computer she worked on was the Mark I, eight feet high and the length of a long room. Over the years, she was an active participant as computers evolved from binary switches to vacuum tubes and finally computer chips. Dedicated to computers and the Navy, she continued to wear her uniform, consult, and give lectures until she was over eighty years old. A feisty, eccentric, brilliant woman, she is an intriguing role model and an inspiration for any child with a knack for computers. While the text is generally accessible for early readers, some of the computer terminology and technology may require explanation.

Grandma Moses: Painter of Rural America, Zibby Oneal, illustrations by Donna Ruff; paintings by Grandma Moses, *1986, United States,* BIOGRAPHY, *58 pages*

Born in 1860, Anna Mary Robertson (later Moses) spent the first seventy years of her life working on farms in eastern New York State and Virginia. While life was hard, there were many happy memories of rural life: tapping maple syrup, sledding down the hills, hunting for Christmas trees, and chasing the Thanksgiving turkey. In the 1930s, Anna Mary, now Grandma Moses, began painting. For the next thirty years she created folk art paintings—brightly colored landscapes that evoked her rural childhood world. Zibby Oneal's simple and well-written biography takes us from Anna Mary's child-hood through her old age and fame. Pencil illustrations and black-and-white reproductions of Grandma Moses's paintings accompany the text, although the reader who wants to appreciate fully this mar-velous painter's work will need to seek out full-color reproductions.

The Hundred Dresses, Eleanor Estes, illustrated by Louis Slobodkin, *1944, United States,* FICTION, *80 pages*

Wanda Petronski lives in the poor part of town and always wears the same clean, faded-blue dress to school. When she tells a group of girls that she has a hundred dresses in her closet, the girls are incredu-lous, and then make her the target of daily teasing. Eventually, Wanda's family leaves. Mr. Petronski writes in a letter to Wanda's class: "Now we move away to big city. No more holler Polack. No more ask why funny name. Plenty of funny names in the big city." Wanda leaves behind an amazing surprise, however. Told through the growing consciousness of Wanda's classmate Maddie, *The Hundred Dresses* contains a strong message about prejudice and the need for understanding.

> *A player should be as good at picking up a book as picking up a baseball.*
>
> *Sam Ricketts, elementary school student*

In the Year of the Boar and Jackie Robinson, Bette Bao Lord, illus-trated by Marc Simont, *1984, United States,* FICTION, *169 pages*

Before she and her mother left China to join her father in the United States, Sixth Cousin was told by Grandfather that she needed an official name. Sixth Cousin knew she wanted an American name;

after discarding Uncle Sam she chose Shirley Temple, and so Shirley Temple Wong was registered in the Clan Book in the thirty-ninth generation. New York City in 1947 leaves Shirley in awe, and fifth grade is very confusing. Using laugh-out-loud humor, filling the book with love of family, piano lessons, and baseball, Betty Bao Lord leads us through Shirley's first year in her adopted country. She lets her readers laugh at Shirley's observations and frustrations, then turns the table on us by revealing a Chinese tale that explains her reactions. This is a fine story of immigration, language, and family, and of one spunky, strong-willed little girl who always rises to the occasion.

Jane Goodall: Living with the Chimps, Julie Fromer, illustrated by Antonio Castro, *1992, Tanzania,* BIOGRAPHY, *69 pages*

Older readers may want to refer to Jane Goodall's autobiography, *Living with Chimps,* but Julie Fromer's biography provides early readers with an informative look into the life of one of the world's foremost primatologists. Jane Goodall knew from an early age that she wanted to observe animals; one of her first memories is sitting hunched in a chicken coop for five hours hoping to see a chicken lay an egg. At twenty-three, she went to Africa for a visit and stayed as an assistant secretary to Louis Leakey, who later got her started on a project observing chimpanzees in the forests of Tanzania. After a year of frustrating attempts, Jane Goodall was finally rewarded with her first encounter with the chimps. More than forty years later, she continues her research and says there is still more to learn.

A Jar of Dreams, Yoshiko Uchida, *1981, United States,* FICTION, *131 pages*

When eleven-year-old Rinko learns that her Aunt Waka is coming from Japan for a visit, Rinko is not certain she is pleased—after all, she'll have to move out of her room and share one with her brother. But Aunt Waka brings something special to Rinko's family, for Aunt Waka believes in herself. While Rinko, who has grown up with discrimination, often feels ashamed of her Japanese heritage, Aunt Waka is proud. When a racist business competitor tries to force

Rinko's family out of their home laundry business, it is Aunt Waka who convinces Rinko's father to confront him. Belief is a powerful thing, and by the end of that summer of 1935, Rinko's entire family has gained the confidence to strive for their dreams.

> *I'll curl up in a chair and read for hours without noticing. Not just happiness flows through me, but a warm feeling of comfort, too.*
>
> Caitlin Bauermeister, elementary school student

Katie and the Lemon Tree, Esther Bender, illustrated by Joy Dunn Keenan, *1994, United States,* FICTION, *89 pages*

Katie and her husband, Daniel, leave their home and family in Germany and set sail for America in hopes of finding land of their own. Katie's mother tells her to keep the faith, and Katie does, although the years are long and busy with activity—building a house, cultivating raw land, growing crops and making maple syrup, and always, always, saving to bring the rest of Katie's family over. When Katie first arrived in Boston, she was given a lemon by a young fruit seller. Even though she has been told that lemons won't grow in this climate, Katie plants its seeds in a small pot. Through the years, she tends the seedling, then tree, inside their house, and it becomes a symbol of her faith. When the tree grows too large, she asks Daniel to build a glass house outside for it. The glass house, and the vegetables and flowers they grow in it, finally give them financial security. A story about spiritual faith and everyday work, *Katie and the Lemon Tree* gives children a fuller understanding of one of Katie's mother's favorite sayings: "Keep the faith and milk the cow."

Katie Henio: Navajo Sheepherder, Peggy Thomson, photographs by Paul Conklin, *1995, United States,* BIOGRAPHY, *51 pages*

Katie Henio loves the out-of-doors, and although she is a great-grandmother and her children wish she was at home more, Katie knows that being with her sheep gives every aspect of her life joy. Listen to her talk about her sheep—their personalities and the care they need. Go with her to harvest plants for food, health, ceremonies, or the dyeing of wool. Sit beside her loom and watch her practiced hands weave an intricate pattern seemingly out of air. Laugh with her as she tells stories about her lazy horse, or Brunt Woman, the sheep that constantly escapes. Learn from her as she tells her grandchildren: "Look back and try to understand, so the past will not leave scars. The past will live as part of you." Katie Henio is a remarkable woman, and this biography, translated from the Navajo into English by Katie Henio's son and chockful of color photographs, is an admirable testament to a woman who lives life with grace, humor, and self-reliance.

> *I love stories. I am devoted to stories. I feel sure that at three I did not ask "Why?" but rather, "Then what happened?" The reason I began to write fiction was not that I believed myself to be one of those enviable artists, the "born storyteller," but that I loved stories so much I wanted to be on the inside.*
>
> Katherine Paterson, *writer*

Katie John, Mary Calhoun, *1960, United States,* FICTION, *134 pages*

Ten-year-old Katie John is stuck in Missouri until her parents can sell the big old house Great-aunt Emily left them when she died. Missouri is *not* California, and this house is not what Katie John has in mind. But the house has a dumbwaiter (well, yes, of course she has to try riding it), trunks with old letters, and walls that talk. A small town is perfect for a lemonade stand, and Sue Halsey lives just three doors down. By the end of the summer, Katie is figuring out a way her family can stay forever. Katie John is a wonderful character, a careless tomboy with great intentions, ready for any adventure. You'll wish she lived three doors down from you.

The King's Equal, Katherine Paterson, illustrated by Vladimir Vagin, *1992, Europe,* FANTASY, *64 pages*

As the king lies dying, he calls his selfish son to his side and proclaims that Prince Raphael can never wear the crown until he marries a woman his equal in intelligence, beauty, and wealth. Good luck, for Raphael's conceit and greed make this almost impossible. After a year of searching, the councilors have given up hope, when a young woman arrives wearing a circlet of gold around her head. Even though she is the daughter of a poor shepherd, she quickly proves that she is more than Raphael's equal, and now it is he who must undergo the test while she rules the kingdom. Katherine Paterson, author of many well-loved books, succeeds in teaching a great deal about true beauty, wisdom, wealth, and gender equality.

The Last Princess: The Story of Princess Ka'iulani of Hawaii, Fay Stanley, illustrated by Diane Stanley, *1991, United States,* BIOGRAPHY, *40 pages*

Mother and daughter Fay and Diane Stanley collaborated on this sympathetic portrayal of the last princess of Hawaii and the annexation of her homeland by white Americans in the late nineteenth century. The story of the princess's idyllic childhood, her education in England, her temporary victory in convincing Grover Cleveland to save her country, and the eventual loss of her country's right to rule itself are described in a straightforward style, accompanied by detailed and richly colored illustrations. While the story of Princess Ka'iulani's life does not end happily or triumphantly, it provides important lessons about the United States' treatment of native peoples and of the need to speak out, whether or not you succeed.

Last Summer with Maizon, Jacqueline Woodson, *1990, United States,* FICTION, *105 pages*

Margaret and Maizon are best friends. They are always together; they even buy the same outfits to wear to school. It's Maizon who understands, who helps Margaret when her father dies of a heart attack. But now Maizon is going off to a fancy school called Blue Hill, and Margaret feels left behind in Brooklyn. What Margaret learns that autumn, however, are the ways friends help and the ways they can hold us back. With Maizon away, Margaret becomes aware of her own talents, and when Maizon returns, their friendship is different and stronger. This lovely book, sad and full of warmth at the same time, teaches about loss and all we may learn within it.

> *"Word," said Jay, pointing to the page.*
> *"Writer," Margaret said, pointing to herself. She turned to a clean page and continued.*
>
> from Last Summer with Maizon *by Jacqueline Woodson*

Linnea in Monet's Garden, Christina Bjork, illustrated by Lena Anderson, *1985, France,* FICTION, *51 pages*

With her all-absorbing interest in Monet and his gardens, whimsical Linnea is the perfect companion for introducing children to the world of Impressionist art. With her elderly friend Mr. Bloom, Linnea makes a pilgrimage to Giverny, Monet's home in France, so that she can sit in his kitchen, stand on the bridge he painted, and see the water lilies for herself. This is a very educational book, filled with photographs of the house, gardens, and Monet's paintings (some of them up close so you can understand Impressionism better). It is also a fun read, following Linnea on her grand adventure with her big straw hat, black leggings, white pinafore, and funny little smile.

Lisa and Lottie, Erich Kästner, illustrated by Walter Trier, *1949, Germany,* FICTION, *137 pages*

Lisa—"a little girl of nine with a head framed in curls and filled with bright ideas"—is at summer camp at Bohrlaken on Lake Bohren. Is she ever surprised when the bus arrives with a new load of girls and the twentieth little girl looks just like Lisa. Lottie is quiet, her hair tightly braided, but the resemblance is extraordinary. It doesn't take too long for the girls to discover they are twins, separated at a young age when their parents divorced. Suddenly, each child has a sister and a parent she didn't know was alive. Before the end of camp, the two girls have decided to switch places. Lisa goes to live with her hardworking single mother in Vienna, and Lottie is off to meet her father, a self-centered but essentially loving conductor and composer. The girls' escapade is filled with humor, as each child tries to avoid detection, and in the end, of course, they bring their parents back together.

> *I hold my books up to memory's light, faces gleam, there are whispers from long ago belonging to old friends. . . . I open the books; the characters stretch and pull me back in.*
>
> *Jill Robinson, writer*

The Little House in the Big Woods, Laura Ingalls Wilder, illustrated by Garth Williams, *1932, United States,* AUTOBIOGRAPHICAL FICTION, *238 pages*

Laura Ingalls Wilder's series of *Little House* books recalls a simpler time, glowing with family love, filled with challenges and adventures, and alive with the charm and spunk of a little girl named Laura. Generations of readers remember the time Ma went out to milk the cow and slapped a bear, and the descriptions of making maple sugar and churning butter. Without hiding the obvious difficulties of pioneer life in the Big Woods of Wisconsin in the 1870s, Laura Ingalls Wilder looks back on her own childhood with affection and humor. Garth Williams's illustrations bring us Ma's gentle face, Pa's long beard and kind eyes, Mary's exasperatingly perfect curls, and Laura's fly-away hair and rambunctious personality. Start with the first in the series and let your children grow along with them, as Laura and her family move progressively westward.

The Little Riders, Margaretha Shemin, illustrated by Peter Spier, *1963, Holland,* FICTION, *76 pages*

Four years ago, Johanna was sent to visit her grandparents in Holland. Soon after, World War II broke out and Johanna was not allowed to return to America. Now eleven, Johanna watches as German troops march through her town and a German officer takes over her bedroom. Mostly, Johanna watches the twelve little riders that hourly come out of the town clock. Rumor has it they will be melted down for ammunition. When the time comes for the villagers to try to save the little riders, it is Johanna and a surprising ally who protect both the little riders and Johanna's grandparents. A story of courage and understanding, it can also serve as an introduction to World War II for those readers not yet ready for more intense books such as *The Devil's Arithmetic*.

Lost Star: The Story of Amelia Earhart, Patricia Lauber, *1988, United States,* BIOGRAPHY, *101 pages*

Amelia Earhart, or "AE" as she liked to be called, was a high-spirited, adventurous gal. She was born in 1897 to parents who exposed her and her sister to dolls and trucks, cooking and fishing. Although they moved frequently and her father drank too much, she grew up with the confidence that she could try anything. After her first airplane ride in 1920, she knew she had to fly. In 1928, sitting in a plane piloted by two men, she became the first woman to "fly" across the Atlantic Ocean. It made her an instant star. She continued setting aviation records, piloting the plane herself, and in 1932 soloed across the Atlantic. Feeling she had one long flight left in her, in 1937 she and navigator Fred Noonan began their flight around the world at the equator. They never returned. Throughout her life, AE believed in equal opportunities for women, and wrote articles and organized women in aviation. An independent and committed woman, she comes alive in this engrossing biography, and the reader understands why, sixty years after her disappearance, she still holds a fascination for many.

Maria: A Christmas Story, Theodore Taylor, *1992, United States,* FICTION, *72 pages*

For as long as eleven-year-old Maria Fuentes Gonzaga can remember, she has watched the rich families plan and then parade their huge Christmas floats down the main street of their town on the first

Saturday of December. Never has anyone in the Mexican-American community, most of them poor farmers, taken part. On the playground one day, Maria boasts that this year her family will have a float. What happens as a result becomes a tradition that you can still see every year in the town of San Lazaro, in California's San Joaquin Valley.

> *Out on the sidewalk, Maria yelled, "You changed your mind, Papa! You changed your mind!" and ran into his arms. He grinned at her. "I'm as crazy as you are."*
>
> *from* Maria: A Christmas Story *by Theodore Taylor*

Mary Marony Hides Out, Suzy Kline, illustrated by Blanche Sims, *1993, United States,* FICTION, *80 pages*

Second-grader Mary Marony is a reader, a writer, and a stutterer, a trait made worse when she is nervous, especially with the letter *m*. She is excited that her favorite author is speaking at her school and surprised when she sees a tall, wild-haired woman wearing men's shoes. Then, in front of the whole school, the author asks Mary her name. All Mary can say is "Muh-muh-muh" until her teacher answers for her. Mary is so embarrassed that she hides out in the bathroom. Later, Mary wins lunch with the author as a prize, but Mary doesn't want to go, sure that the author thinks she is stupid because of her stuttering. It is at lunch that Mary learns she is not the only one who has had apprehensions about herself. In *Mary Marony Hides Out*, we meet one child, and through the story, others who overcome a difference made worse by fear. Mary's frustration rings true, and Suzy Kline's entertaining writing offers hope and insight.

Mary McLeod Bethune: Voice of Black Hope, Milton Meltzer, illustrated by Stephen Marchesi, *1987, United States,* BIOGRAPHY, *57 pages*

Mary grew up in a family of seventeen children, the McLeods' first free-born child. Part of a hardworking family, she helped plow the fields and pick the cotton, but always she wanted to learn how to read. When the chance came for one child in the family to go to school, the McLeods picked Mary. Mary walked the five miles to and from school every day; in the evenings, she taught her siblings what she had learned. After attending a seminary in North Carolina, she applied to be a missionary in Africa, only to be turned down because she was black. She found her life work in her own country—teaching and starting schools for black children. The small school she started in 1904 evolved into Bethune-Cookman College, and Mary became a driving force in creating opportunities and resources for black people throughout the country. Milton Meltzer makes Mary McLeod Bethune's life accessible and interesting for younger readers, without oversimplifying the numerous accomplishments of this remarkable woman.

Mary Poppins, P. L. Travers, illustrated by Mary Shepard, *1934, England,* FICTION, *206 pages*

Forget Disney, forget Julie Andrews, nice as she is. The original Mary Poppins is the best, with her pointy nose, bossy manner, and delightful adventures. When Mary Poppins arrives at the Banks residence in response to an ad for a nanny, it is the Banks family that must pass approval, not Mary Poppins. But don't think she is stuffy, or that life will be boring. There are sidewalk pictures that come to life, laughing gas that makes you float—and only Mary Poppins can really understand what dogs and birds say. A strict disciplinarian who slides up the banisters, properly British and full of surprises, she keeps the children enthralled until she flies away with the West Wind. Those who love her know she will return.

Matilda, Roald Dahl, illustrated by Quentin Blake, *1988, England,* FICTION, *240 pages*

Matilda Wormwood is a brilliant little girl cursed with the stupidest, crassest parents in England. Her father wears a cheap toupee and sells used cars; her mother is addicted to television. The only person who seems to realize the range of Matilda's intelligence is her teacher, Miss Honey, but Miss Honey is ruled over by the principal,

Miss Trunchbull. If Mr. and Mrs. Wormwood are disgusting, Miss Trunchbull is terrifying—a huge, hulking woman who slings children about by their hair and has her teachers cowering. Matilda's triumph over "the Trunchbull" raises cheers from readers and Matilda's fellow students. Some grown-ups may wince at the completely incorrect behavior of parents and principal, but children relish this world of good and evil, where the lines are clear, good is young, and success is certain.

> *My favorite character is Matilda because she can shoot power out of her eyes and she loves to read like me.*
> *Alison Sargent, elementary school student*

Meet Posy Bates, Helen Cresswell, illustrated by Kate Aldous, *1992, England,* FICTION, *95 pages*

Posy Bates is a British Ramona the Pest, full of quirky ideas and good intentions, most of which backfire. The plot loosely follows eight-year-old Posy's dream of having a pet and her attempts to convince her mother to let her get one. Plot isn't what carries you through this magical book, however; it's the incidents that happen along Posy's circuitous path to achieving her goal. There are several enchanting encounters with a bag lady, Posy's elaborate educational conversations with her baby brother, a hilarious and disastrous Sunday afternoon with Posy's four-year-old cousin, an equally funny capture of a wildly flea-ridden hedgehog, and a pet show that turns into complete pandemonium. Posy's energy is contagious, and the incidents happen at a speed and level of excitement that is sure to keep early readers turning the pages long after lights-out.

Morning Girl, Michael Dorris, *1992, Bahamas,* HISTORICAL FICTION, *80 pages*

This story is told through the voices of a twelve-year-old Morning Girl and her young brother Star Boy, two Taino children living on a peaceful island in the Bahamas just prior to its "discovery" by

Christopher Columbus. Star Boy likes to be awake at night; Morning Girl got her name "because I wake up early, always with something on my mind. Mother says it's because I dream too hard." While it seems these two will never agree, events occur that put their conflicts in a new light. *Morning Girl* is a lyrically written book about growing up, learning to love a sibling, and finding your place in the world. The gentleness and wisdom of the Taino people is set in ironic contrast with the coming of white men and a quote from Christopher Columbus, who sees these people as "good and intelligent servants."

> *When I was about eight, I decided the most wonderful thing, next to a human being, was a book.*
>
> *Margaret Walker, writer*

Mrs. Piggle-Wiggle, Betty MacDonald, illustrated by Hilary Knight, *1947, United States,* FICTION, *119 pages*

Children fight over which of the many Mrs. Piggle-Wiggle books is their favorite; the truth is, they are all wonderful. Try starting with the first, which introduces you to Mrs. Piggle-Wiggle herself, who lives in an upside-down house and has a magic hump ("a convenient fastening place for wings"). She has no children, but the entire neighborhood plays at her house, and when parents are at their wit's end, they call Mrs. Piggle-Wiggle and receive advice which, while sometimes unorthodox, always works. Patsy won't wash? Well, let the dirt accumulate and when it is deep enough, plant radish seeds. Some solutions are so commonsense you'll want to try them yourself, others are simply magical and hilarious. It's a toss-up who enjoys this book more, children or adults—certainly it's a great one to read aloud.

My Name Is María Isabel, Alma Flor Ada, illustrated by Dyble K. Thompson, *1993, United States,* FICTION, *57 pages*

María Isabel recently moved from Puerto Rico to the United States. Now she has to move again, and it's hard for her to have to change schools. In her new class there are two other Marias and the teacher decides to call María Isabel Mary. María Isabel is named for her two grandmothers and she loves and draws strength from her name. Mary? Who is that? she wonders. At her other school, lessons were taught in Spanish and English, but this class is only in English, so María Isabel has to pay very close attention. Sometimes she forgets that she is called Mary and that causes problems. Grow with María Isabel as she makes friends at school, becomes comfortable in her neighborhood, and finds a way to tell her teacher that her name is María Isabel.

Naya Nuki: The Girl Who Ran, Kenneth Thomasma, illustrated by Eunice Hundley, *1983, United States,* BIOGRAPHICAL FICTION, *131 pages*

Shoshoni Indians Naya Nuki and her friend Sacajawea need to hunt in enemy territory for buffalo—food is scarce and the hides are needed for clothing. Then one morning the Minnetare Indians attack. Many Shoshonis die and the two eleven-year-old girls are among those captured. Immediately, Naya Nuki begins to plan her escape, memorizing landmarks on the forty-one-day walk to the Minnetare village. Sacajawea is afraid of fleeing, so on a rainy, moonless night, Naya Nuki runs away alone from the village and begins a journey of more than one thousand miles back to her people. It is dangerous, and Naya Nuki must use all her knowledge for survival, for she must reach home before winter arrives. Her determination is tested repeatedly as she runs low on food, becomes ill, and must stay off traveled paths for fear of being recaptured. Based on an actual incident that occurred in 1801, this remarkable story is told with excitement, compassion, and respect.

Nightjohn, Gary Paulsen, *1993, United States,* FICTION, *92 pages*

Sarny is a slave girl living on the Waller plantation on the day they bring in a new slave named Nightjohn, shackled by the neck, his back covered with scars from whippings. Sarny learns Nightjohn ran away once and got to the North, but he returned to teach slaves how to read at the risk of being captured. Nightjohn may be a slave once more, but he is not done teaching. When Sarny and Nightjohn start drawing letters in the dust, they take a terrible risk: it's illegal to teach a slave how to read. The costs are horribly high, and Sarny tells them in her no-nonsense, often anger-filled voice. *Nightjohn* is a graphic, moving story about injustice and triumph, a powerful and important book that adults may want to read alongside young readers.

> *It was in the flower bed that I first heard about Nightjohn. Not by name, but by happening.*
>
> *from* Nightjohn *by Gary Paulsen*

Nothing Is Impossible: The Story of Beatrix Potter, Dorothy Aldis, illustrated by Richard Cuffari, *1969, England,* BIOGRAPHY, *156 pages*

Beatrix Potter is best known for her well-loved children's books, among them *The Tales of Benjamin Bunny* and *Peter Rabbit*. The story of her life is far less well-known, but is fantastic in its own right. Beatrix Potter grew up in London, the daughter of wealthy if distant parents, and spent most of her time on the third floor of their house. Though she had few human contacts, she was fascinated by watercolor painting, the Kensington Museum, and the various small animals in her pet menagerie. When she was older, Beatrix began to make up stories for the children of her former French tutor. Eventually the stories turned into books, and by her late thirties, Beatrix had made enough money to buy her own farm. This is the story of the talent, strength, and dedication of a young girl who grows up to be an eccentric and wonderful woman.

Onion Tears, Diana Kidd, illustrated by Lucy Montgomery, *1989, Australia,* FICTION, *62 pages*

When Nam-Huong cuts onions, her "eyes sting and pour tears like monsoon rains." What Nam-Huong would like to do is cry real tears for the many losses she has suffered. It's difficult living in Australia with Auntie, a woman who is watching her until Nam-Huong is, hopefully, reunited with her parents in Vietnam, for Nam-Huong's heart and mind are always wondering about the family she left behind. At school, kids make fun of her because she doesn't talk. Instead, she writes letters to her best friends back home—the yellow canary and the little duck—and through the letters she reveals her past. Soldiers forced her father from their home and, at her mother's insistence, Nam-Huong and her grandfather took a long, treacherous boat ride. Grandfather died and left Nam-Huong to arrive in Australia alone. Nam-Huong's story raises important issues of what it's like to be an outsider and afraid. With the help of another refugee who makes Nam-Huong laugh, and a gentle, generous teacher, Nam-Huong learns to trust and love again.

> *"My child," said the Fairy Crustacea, "I am going to give you something that will probably bring you more happiness than all these fall-lals and fripperies put together. You shall be Ordinary!"*
> *from* The Ordinary Princess *by M. M. Kaye*

The Ordinary Princess, M. M. Kaye, author and illustrator, *1980, Europe,* FANTASY, *112 pages*

Amy is the seventh princess of Phantasmorania, given the gift of ordinariness by a disgruntled fairy invited to her christening. Rather than "marry some stupid dragon-slaying prince," Amy runs away and, after living happily in the woods for a while, ends up a kitchen maid in the castle of the king of Ambergeldar. There she meets a young man who calls himself a "man-of-all-work." Their friendship quickly develops until—didn't you see it coming?—each finds out the other is royalty. There are many books that propose to do a twist on traditional princess fairy tales, but few do it with such wit and fun. Amy is a marvelous human being who loves the woods and the concept of earning her own living, and her relationship with her man-of-all-work is a solid and satisfying one.

Philip Hall likes me. I reckon maybe. Bette Greene, illustrated by Charles Lilly, *1974, United States,* FICTION, *139 pages*

This warm and funny book is told in eleven-year-old Beth Lambert's down-to-earth, high-spirited voice. Beth is quick and sharp, second in her class only to Philip Hall, her friend and the object of her considerable affection. The problem is, Beth likes to win—she even thinks she could probably be first in their class—but she doesn't want Philip to be mad at her. As Beth goes through her eleventh year—catching turkey thieves, selling vegetables to raise money for college, picketing bigoted Mr. Puttenham's store, rescuing Philip, raising a 4-H calf—she, and Philip, learn about winning, self-esteem, and friendship.

Phoebe the Spy, Judith Berry Griffin, illustrated by Margot Tomes, *1977, United States,* BIOGRAPHY, *46 pages*

One little-known piece of Revolutionary War history belongs to Phoebe Fraunces, a free African-American girl who saved George Washington's life. Phoebe's father ran the Fraunces Tavern, where many army officers congregated in New York City. One day, Phoebe's father learned of a plot to kill General Washington, and asked his thirteen-year-old daughter to serve as a housemaid in the General's house in the hopes of finding out more information. In the end, Phoebe not only spied, but, through her quick thinking, kept the General from being poisoned. It's a fascinating and suspenseful story, overladen with irony—for Phoebe and her father are both aware that she is protecting the life of a man who means to liberate a country, yet who keeps slaves himself.

Pippi Longstocking, Astrid Lindgren, illustrated by Louis S. Glanzman, *1950, Sweden,* FICTION, *160 pages*

If you were nine years old, had a suitcase full of gold coins, lived in your own home with a pet monkey and horse (and no parents), and were the strongest girl in the world, what do you think your life would be like? Meet Pippi Longstocking—she used to travel the seas with her father and has been to Egypt, Africa, India, and China, just to name a few places, so she knows things other kids don't. She also tells lies—they make a story more interesting—and she entertains herself and two neighbor children with her adventures and stories. Let yourself get carried away with Pippi as she rescues the policemen who are stuck on her roof, goes to the circus, and dances with burglars. Kindhearted and determined, Pippi is worthy of admiration.

> *I like to read in my bed because it feels as if I can be in my book where the action is. It feels like the book is my room.*
> Tyler Helbach, *elementary school student*

The Princess and the Admiral, Charlotte Pomerantz, illustrated by Tony Chen, *1974, Vietnam,* FOLKLORE, *48 pages*

Princess Mat Mat is proud that there has been no war for nearly one hundred years in the Tiny Kingdom. Just when Mat Mat is to decide the date for the celebration of peace, her three advisors tell her that warships are moving toward the kingdom. From the information the court astrologer gives her, Mat Mat devises a clever way to defeat the incoming ships without the loss of life. The Admiral falls right into her trap; when the fisherfolk throw chickens, pots, coconuts, and anything else handy at his fleet, he thinks them a rather primitive people and decides to conquer them in the morning. Mat Mat knows the moon and the tides are in her favor, and by morning the Admiral is at her mercy. Based on the legend of Kublai Khan's naval invasion of Vietnam in the thirteenth century, *The Princess and the Admiral* is an entertaining and humorous story.

Queenie Peavy, Robert Burch, illustrated by Jerry Lazare, *1966, United States,* FICTION, *159 pages*

It's the 1930s in Georgia and times are tough for everybody, especially for Queenie Peavy and her mom, with Queenie's dad in jail for robbery. It's hard for Queenie to keep her anger under control when she is teased about her dad by kids at school. But Queenie, with her thirteen-year-old's independent streak, is also smart and funny. Told from Queenie's perspective, this is her story of visits to the principal's office, of singing while she does her night chores, of false accusations and the painful lessons Queenie learns when her dad gets out of jail. There are some hard knocks and bruises along the way, but also some kind hands and words, and when the book is done, Queenie still has sparkle in her spirit.

Rachel Carson Who Loved the Sea, Jean Lee Latham, illustrated by Victor Mays, *1973, United States,* BIOGRAPHY, *80 pages*

Rachel Carson grew up knowing she loved to write; at college, she discovered biology. In her career, her two interests came together. At first, she worked for the Bureau of Fisheries, writing radio stories about the sea; eventually, she became one of their first women scientists. Encouraged by those who loved her articles to write longer works, Rachel Carson created several critically acclaimed and widely popular books about the ocean. Toward the end of her life, knowing she was dying from cancer, Rachel Carson wrote what many consider her most important work, *Silent Spring.* Published in 1958, it was one of the first real warnings about the dangers of pesticides. Jean Latham's easy-to-read biography shows us a hardworking and caring woman dedicated to her family and to nature.

> *I am sure I read every book of fairy tales in our branch library, with one complaint—all that long golden hair. Never mind—my short brown hair became long and golden as I read and when I grew up I would write a book about a brown-haired girl to even things up.*
>
> Beverly Cleary, writer

Ramona the Pest, Beverly Cleary, illustrated by Lois Darling, *1968, United States,* FICTION, *192 pages*

You can't go wrong with a book by Beverly Cleary; she remembers what it was like to be a child, and she captures it on every page. Ramona is spunky, careless, full of imagination, often in trouble, and—in this book—entering kindergarten. Ramona's Qs have tails and whiskers; for Ramona, a pink worm becomes an engagement ring. And how is she supposed to resist boinging Susan's incredibly tempting curls? This is a funny, sympathetic look at being five and at all the awkward times that can come with it, one in a series of vastly popular books.

Ransom for a River Dolphin, Sarita Kendall, *1992, Colombia,* FICTION, *123 pages*

Along the Amazon River, dolphins, especially pink ones, are considered sacred animals by many of the local Indian people. When Carmenza and her friend Ramiro find a badly injured pink dolphin, they know it is their duty to help it heal. Guided by Ramiro's father, the children learn much about nature as they care for the dolphin. But Carmenza has other concerns too: Was her stepfather responsible for the dolphin's injuries? Is her baby brother's illness related to the sick dolphin? Are the two strangers gathering animals from the forest bringing bad luck to the village? As readers find the answers to these questions, they learn about the Ticuna and Witoto Indians who live along the Amazon banks, as well as about friendship, dolphin folklore, and the cost of greed.

A Ride on the Red Mare's Back, Ursula K. Le Guin, illustrated by Julie Downing, *1992, Europe,* FANTASY, *48 pages*

This is a story of fantasy, of trolls and magic wooden toy horses, of a kidnapped little boy and his sister who sets out to rescue him. With only her toy horse, a red scarf, a pair of knitting needles, and some bread, she walks out into the snowy night. When she is threatened by a troll, the toy horse comes to life, but only for one night. The rest is magic—sometimes scary, sometimes funny—lyrically told. Fans of Ursula Le Guin's books for adults can share their enthusiasm through this natural read-aloud; young readers will find this a good introduction to the wonder of her writing.

Rigoberto Menchú, Caroline Lazo, *1994, Guatemala,* BIOGRAPHY, *61 pages*

Rigoberto Menchú won the Nobel Peace Prize in 1992 for her continuing efforts for peace between the majority Indian tribes and the ruling Spanish-speaking minority of Guatemala. The military government has given the Indians little access to education, discouraged them from practicing their Mayan religion, and taken their land. Rigoberto Menchú was born in 1959; one of nine children in her Quiche Indian family, she began picking coffee beans at the age of eight to help supplement her family's income. Raised speaking her native language, she came to realize the importance of speaking Spanish and taught herself. Words have become her weapon in her struggle to overthrow the government. Despite horrific injustices against her family and the Indian majority, and conflict with another Indian faction that supports violent means to ending the government's rule, Rigoberto remains committed to a nonviolent resolution. Using many photographs and direct quotes from Rigoberto Menchú's autobiography, Caroline Lazo has created a memorable, accessible biography of this amazing peacemaker.

Roller Skates, Ruth Sawyer, illustrated by Valenti Angelo, *1936, United States,* FICTION, *186 pages*

Ten-year-old Lucinda's parents have gone to Europe and left her behind for a year with her teacher, Miss Peters. Lucinda is a whirlwind of activity, imagination, and energy, and now for the first time she can allow her personality free rein. It is the late 1890s, and New York City is still a place where a child can roller-skate alone for miles, and where policemen, hansom cab drivers, fruit stand vendors, rag peddlers, thespians, and candy shop owners make easy and affectionate friends. Lucinda has enough love and admiration to encompass a whole world of people, and enough spirit to get into some perfectly awful situations when she has no physical release and she feels "the lid of the box begin to press down upon her." Passionate, unruly, willing to give away her most treasured possessions for the joy of making someone else happy, she is a delightful companion.

Rosa Bonheur, Robyn Montana Turner, *1991, France,* BIOGRAPHY, *32 pages*

Robyn Montana Turner has produced a series of biographies of women artists, including Georgia O'Keeffe, Frida Kahlo, and Mary Cassatt. Simple and basic in their narratives, teeming with color reproductions, photographs, and sketches, they are appropriate for early readers wishing to do independent research. The biography of Rosa Bonheur, born in France in 1822, provides one of the most interesting reading experiences, largely because of Rosa Bonheur's personality and life story. As the young child of a painter, she was encouraged to experiment with her art—on the living-room walls, if she liked. As an adolescent, she learned art in her father's studio and during hours spent in the Louvre. Her particular interest was animals, which she painted in a precise and remarkably realistic style. Her work gained her both critical acclaim and financial success. Rosa Bonheur eventually bought a chateau where she lived a happy and productive existence with her lifelong friend Nathalie Micas and a huge menagerie of pets, including cows, deer, gazelles, and even lions.

> *Idle hands were "trouble" when I was growing up. But if you were reading you were in good graces and could hide away half the day—which I did.*
>
> *Maxine Schuler, master gardener*

Sadako and the Thousand Paper Cranes, Eleanor Coerr, paintings by Ronald Himler, *1977, Japan,* BIOGRAPHICAL FICTION, *64 pages*

Swift, energetic, eleven-year-old Sadako races to the park for Hiroshima Peace Day, a celebration to remember all who died in the atomic blast ten years before. Within weeks Sadako feels dizzy, an all-too-familiar sign of leukemia. She decides not to tell anyone, but soon it is obvious something is wrong. While Sadako is in the hospital, a friend teaches her how to make an origami paper crane and reminds her that legend says if a sick person makes a thousand cranes, the gods will make her well. With each crane Sadako folds, she feels courage to carry on and makes a wish to get better. She is able to make 644 before she dies from leukemia like so many other survivors of the blast. Her classmates fold 356 more and all 1,000 are buried with her. Today there is a statue of Sadako in the Hiroshima Peace Park and each year on Peace Day, thousands of cranes are laid at its base. Eleanor Coerr does not mask the sadness of Sadako's story, but there is also optimism in the love of Sadako's family and community, renewed with the importance of remembering.

Sarah, Plain and Tall, Patricia MacLachlan, *1985, United States,* FICTION, *58 pages*

There is something beautifully spare and poetic about Patricia MacLachlan's writing; it comforts and inspires you like a wise, loving friend. *Sarah, Plain and Tall* tells the story of a nineteenth-century Midwestern widower who advertises for a new wife and mother for his two children. Sarah responds from Maine, telling them of her love of painting and the sea, of her need for new possibilities. When Sarah arrives for a month's trial, their worlds intersect and become enriched. Sarah holds true to her claim that she is her own person. She learns how to ride a horse and drive a wagon; she insists on wearing Papa's overalls if she wants, and on helping to fix the broken roof. When she misses the sea, Papa and the children show her a haystack to serve as a sand dune and shyly offer their affection. In return, Sarah gives them love and, in her own way, brings them the sea.

> *My favorite place to read is in the window seat of my sailboat. . . . Sitting on the dark green cushions, a book propped open on my knees, I feel like I am curled up inside a nut.*
>
> *Migael Scherer, writer*

Sarah's Boat: A Young Girl Learns the Art of Sailing, Douglas Alvord, author and illustrator, *1994, United States,* FICTION, *38 pages*

Shy Sarah loves the summer on the small Maine cove where she lives. That's when she can take her dinghy out and let the sea breeze, her sailing skills, and her imagination carry her away. With her grandfather's encouragement and guidance, Sarah has become quite a sailor. During the summer of her twelfth year, she and Grandpa fix up an old sloop for her with his advice: "You've got to put a little work in her yourself, so she'll know she's yours. Boats have spirits, you know, and you got to take care of them." Many color-pencil drawings of Sarah and her adventures accompany the story. There are also line drawings of boats, identifying parts and giving visual representations of sailing terms—how to tack, do an "S" jibe downwind, use sight bearings to chart your compass course. When Sarah enters the Labor Day race, determined to win, the outcome seems obvious, yet more important is the understanding the reader gains of Sarah's accomplishment, with both her boat and herself.

Scooter, Vera B. Williams, author and illustrator, *1993, United States,* FICTION, *147 pages*

Elana Rose Rosen and her mother are moving into apartment 8E in the Melon Hill Houses in New York City. The city is new for Elana; there are the buildings, the river, city lights, and lots of people to meet. There's Petey, who doesn't talk (but Elana knows he will), Jimmy Beck, who likes to boss people around, and Mrs. Greiner, who strings beads and watches Petey. There are big sidewalks for scooter riding and elevators and . . . it seems the pages can hardly contain everything in Elana's life that summer. Each short chapter starts with a hand-printed acrostic, and whimsical, energetic drawings dance about the pages as young Elana Rose Rosen documents the ups and downs of her new and exciting life.

The Secret of Roan Inish (also titled *The Secret of Ron Mor Skerry*), Rosalie K. Fry, *1985, Ireland,* FANTASY, *89 pages*

The Secret of Roan Inish takes us to an Irish world of islands and seals, myths and belief, old ways and new. The McConvilles lived on the island of Ron Mor for generations until Fiona's father moved their family to the mainland. Before they could go, however, Fiona's little brother Jamie, still in his cradle, was pulled out to sea by the tide. Now several years later, Fiona has been sent to stay with her grandparents, who had to leave Ron Mor but still live by the sea. Fiona knows she can find Jamie and she misses Ron Mor with all her heart. Her longing, the stories she hears, and the power of belief thread their way through this lovely, mystical book.

> *These are not books, lumps of lifeless paper, but* minds *alive on the shelves. From each of them goes out its own voice.*
>
> Gilbert Highet, *writer*

Selma, Lord, Selma: Childhood Memories of the Civil-Rights Days, Sheyann Webb and Rachel West Nelson as told to Frank Sikora, *1980, United States,* MEMOIR, *146 pages*

In January 1965, Sheyann Webb was eight years old; her friend Rachel West was nine. They lived in the houses next door to the Brown Chapel AME Church, the spiritual and logistical center for the Civil Rights protests that eventually led to the historic march from Selma to Montgomery. Sheyann knew early on she wanted to participate; without her parents' knowledge, she skipped school and marched day after day to City Hall as black people attempted to register to vote. Although Rachel was not allowed to join at first, soon their entire community was involved. Taking part in the protests, the girls faced violence, hatred, cold nights, and rain during a three-month period of marching, praying, and singing. Both knew Dr. King; both were close friends of a young white minister who was killed. Their alternating stories, related to Frank Sikora ten years after the march, are stirring and inspiring.

Shark Lady: True Adventures of Eugenie Clark, Ann McGovern, illustrated by Ruth Chew, *1978, United States,* BIOGRAPHY, *83 pages*

As a child, Eugenie Clark often spent her Saturdays at the aquarium in New York City, and there she became fascinated with fish. The tiny apartment she shared with her mother and grandmother was soon filled with fish tanks, as well as salamanders, toads, and even dead rats (for dissection). When she read about a scientist who could stay underwater using a diving helmet, she became determined to swim with the fish herself one day. After college, Eugenie began a career studying fish; she swam with sharks, started her own research station, and became a famous scientist. Written in an easily accessible style, *Shark Lady* illuminates both the intense dedication and the fascinating work of Eugenie Clark.

Sidewalk Story, Sharon Bell Mathis, illustrated by Leo Carty, *1971, United States,* FICTION, *72 pages*

Young Lilly Etta Allen sits on her front stoop one day and sees men moving furniture out of the apartment building across the street. When Lilly Etta recognizes her best friend Tanya's bed, however, and learns that Tanya's family is being evicted and their belongings will be left unprotected on the sidewalk, she gets involved. Determined to help, she takes her carefully hoarded nickels and calls the police and newspaper, but everyone says that this is an ordinary occurrence. It doesn't even matter that Tanya's mother has seven children she is trying to raise by herself. Still, Lilly Etta won't give up, and her sympathy, loyalty, and eventual success show readers the difference one child can make.

> *As a child I felt that books were holy objects, to be caressed, rapturously sniffed, and devotedly provided for. I gave my life to them—I still do. I continue to do what I did as a child: dream of books, make books, and collect books.*
>
> *Maurice Sendak, writer*

The Sign on Rosie's Door, Maurice Sendak, author and illustrator, *1960, United States,* FICTION, *46 pages*

Rosie is a little girl with a nonstop imagination. The sign on her door says to knock three times and she'll tell you a secret. Knock one day and you'll meet Alinda, the famous lady singer; next time Rosie is forlorn Alinda, the lost girl. Rosie's friends—Kathy, Dolly, Sal, and Pudgy—watch and participate with the full range of animated faces that have made Maurice Sendak one of the best-loved of children's illustrators. The children's games are joyful and creative, and when at the end of the book they all decide to become firecrackers for the Fourth of July, it's a gleeful, noisy, deliriously rambunctious celebration.

> *I slid my back down the tree's shaggy trunk and looked up at its long branches, heavy with sweet nuts and slender green leaves, perfectly still. I looked at the leaves of the other trees. They were still also. I stared at the trees, aware of an eerie silence descending over the forest.*
>
> *Stacey walked toward me. "What's the matter with you, Cassie?" he asked.*
>
> *"The trees, Stacey," I said softly, "they ain't singing no more."*
>
> from Song of the Trees *by Mildred D. Taylor*

Song of the Trees, Mildred D. Taylor, illustrated by Jerry Pinkney, 1975, United States, FICTION, 51 pages

Cassie's father has gone to Louisiana to work on the railroads; it's the Depression and there's little work for black men in Mississippi. While he is gone, white Mr. Anderson comes and bullies Cassie's grandmother into giving him permission to cut down the beautiful, ancient trees on their land, trees that Cassie swears she hears sing. Now, as if they know the danger they are in, the trees have stopped singing, as Mr. Anderson first marks and then has his men begin to cut down the trees. It takes four days before Cassie's older brother can bring their father home, and by then many trees have been felled, but in a dramatic and thrilling stand, Cassie's father saves the rest. Based on a real incident, *Song of the Trees* teaches readers the importance of standing up for all that is endangered—whether that be trees, civil rights, or self-respect.

Sophie Hits Six, Dick King-Smith, illustrated by David Parkins, 1991, England, FICTION, 127 pages

The author of the delightful Sophie series was a dairy farmer for twenty years, and used his wife as a model for young Sophie, a "small but determined" girl, dead set on becoming a "lady farmer." Sophie is a solid little presence poised against the freewheeling spontaneity of her older twin brothers, a self-declared tomboy who scorns what she sees as the frivolity of her female classmates. What matters to Sophie is getting a farm, while in the meantime collecting as many animals as possible. In *Sophie's Tom* she gets a cat; in *Sophie Hits Six*, she has acquired a rabbit as well, and has aimed her formidable sights on a puppy.

The Story of Holly and Ivy, Rumer Godden, illustrated by Barbara Cooney, *1957, England,* FANTASY, *32 pages*

"This is a story about wishing"—the wish of a young orphan named Ivy for a family, the wish of a doll named Holly for a little girl of her own, Mrs. Jones's wish to spend Christmas with a child. The wishes cause Ivy—bound from the orphanage to the Infants' Home for Christmas because no one else will take her—to get off the train early in the town of Aylesbury. They inspire Mrs. Jones to buy a Christmas tree, even though she has no children. They encourage Holly to believe she will get a child, even after the stores close on Christmas Eve. Somehow, in the magic that suffuses Rumer Godden's doll stories, anything can happen, and somehow Holly, Ivy, and Mrs. Jones manage to miss, come close to, and finally find each other in time for Christmas breakfast in this wonderfully complicated and completely satisfying story.

Susan Butcher: Sled Dog Racer, Ginger Wadsworth, *1994, United States,* BIOGRAPHY, *63 pages*

From the time she was a child, Susan Butcher knew she hated the city and loved animals, particularly dogs. After high school, she headed to Colorado, where she worked as a veterinary technician until she learned about the Iditarod race in Alaska, a grueling 1,049-mile dog-sled race. Susan moved to Alaska and began working at whatever jobs she could find to earn the money to buy and train her dogs. In the winters, she lived in a remote cabin without electricity or running water, fifty miles from the nearest dirt road. The closeness she established with her dogs paid off and in 1986, Susan became the second woman to win the Iditarod. She went on to win three more times. Ginger Wadsworth's biography takes us into Susan's world: her love of animals, the financial strain and daily work of caring for two hundred dogs, and the suspenseful and life-endangering challenges of running the Iditarod.

> *I read them all, sometimes with shivers of puzzlement and sometimes with delight, but always calling for more. I began to inhabit a world that was two-thirds letterpress and only one-third trees, fields, streets and people.*
>
> H. L. Mencken, *writer*

Thimble Summer, Elizabeth Enright, author and illustrator, *1938, United States,* FICTION, *136 pages*

Thimble Summer takes you back to a Wisconsin farm in the 1930s. It is summer, it is hot, and Garnet is hoping that something exciting will happen. When she finds a silver thimble in the river-bank, she is sure her wish will come true. And it does. It finally rains, her father gets a loan to replace their barn, her family adopts an orphan who wanders onto their property, Garnet gets locked in the library by accident, and her pig wins a prize at the fair. None of these incidents is earth-shattering; all shimmer with the warmth of a Midwestern summer. Garnet is a headstrong, loving young girl; she makes a good companion, whatever the season.

To Hell with Dying, Alice Walker, illustrated by Catherine Deeter, *1967, United States,* MEMOIR, *30 pages*

When Alice Walker was growing up, one of the constants in her life was Mr. Sweet—a gentle, white-haired, often-drinking, guitar-playing neighbor. In this story, she re-creates her memories of her friend—the songs he would play of his sad life, his haircuts and wrinkles, the times she and her siblings would be called upon to tickle and kiss him back to life as he lay on his deathbed. It seemed they would always succeed, their power as magical as Mr. Sweet himself. Finally, when Alice is older, the magic fails, but even then, she learns something. Originally a short story for adults, *To Hell with Dying* works wonderfully for young readers, teaching them about the power of acceptance and love.

Toughboy and Sister, Kirkpatrick Hill, *1990, United States,* FICTION, *121 pages*

Through the long Yukon winter in their Athabascan village, Sister and her brother Toughboy looked forward to going to their summer fishing camp with their father. After their mother's death the previous fall, Dad has continued to binge drink, and they hope he won't at the camp, but he does, and another tragedy follows. Alone for the summer, Sister and Toughboy learn to take care of themselves. At eleven, Toughboy thinks he has to protect his little sister, but he comes to depend on her quick mind to solve problems and on her storytelling to help ease the loneliness. Eight-year-old Sister sees her brother finally let go of his tough image. More than a survival story, *Toughboy and Sister* is an endearing tale of love and co-operation between a sister and brother, in which both the harshness of the climate and the richness of the culture ring true.

> *We read books to find out who we are. What other people, real or imaginary, do and think and feel . . . is an essential guide to our understanding of what we ourselves are and may become.*
> *Ursula K. Le Guin, writer*

The Trail on Which They Wept: The Story of a Cherokee Girl, Dorothy and Thomas Hoobler, illustrated by S. S. Burrus, *1992, United States,* BIOGRAPHICAL FICTION, *53 pages*

When young Sarah Tsaluh Rogers hears rumors that she and the other Cherokees may be forced from their Georgia homeland, she talks with her grandmother, a *ghighua,* or respected elder who keeps alive Cherokee traditions. Her grandmother reminds Tsaluh that she has "the gift to see things that have not yet been and make them come true," and with that gift comes the responsibility of keeping to the Cherokee ways. The soldiers come and force Sarah Tsaluh's family and thousands of other Cherokees to walk to Oklahoma, a long and difficult journey that will become known as the Trail of Tears. Along the trail, Sarah Tsaluh tries to reconcile the wisdom of her grandmother and the Cherokee ways with the teachings of her white school in Georgia. She watches her people suffer, and although her grandmother warns her that she is going to die, Sarah Tsaluh is sad and angry when it happens. With keen interest and a sympathetic heart, the reader journeys with Sarah Tsaluh from her homeland to the Indian territory, and eventually to herself.

Tye May and the Magic Brush, Molly Garrett Bang, author and illustrator, *1981, China,* FOLKLORE, *56 pages*

Orphaned Tye May wants more than anything to learn how to paint. When she asks a teacher if she may borrow a brush to learn, he responds, "Beggar girls don't paint." But Tye May is resourceful; she draws animals in the dirt with sticks, and paints fish on rocks with her wet fingers. In a dream one night, a woman gives her a magic paintbrush and tells Tye May to use it carefully. Tye May wakes up holding a paintbrush. She finds that everything she paints with it becomes real, and she uses her magic brush to help other poor people. Soon the evil Emperor wants her brush. *Tye May* is an ancient Chinese folktale of a girl who is clever in her resolve. The many brushstroke illustrations make *Tye May* a fine read-aloud book; its simple chapter format makes it a good choice for early independent readers.

Understood Betsy, Dorothy Canfield Fisher, *1917, United States,* FICTION, *181 pages*

Betsy has spent her first nine years with her Aunt Frances and grandmother. Aunt Frances "understands" Betsy, shepherds her to school, sympathizes with her every fear. But when Aunt Frances's mother becomes ill, fragile little Betsy is sent to those "horrid Putney cousins" in Vermont. Life there is a revelation for Betsy. As soon as she steps off the train, she is handed the reins to the horses and told she can drive the wagon herself. At the house, she is expected to help, and no one even thinks about walking her to school. While Betsy is mortified at first, she soon delights in her growing independence and self-sufficiency. Taking its inspiration from Montessori theories of parenting and education, *Understood Betsy* is a lesson for both parents and children.

> *On family river trips I take a book up to the red rocks and find a seat in the sun. I sit down. The desert is hot. I shade my book and start to read, but not always. Sometimes I just sit and watch the things around me, like the rapids in the rivers and the canyon wrens flying and singing their beautiful songs.*
>
> *Madeline Rovira, elementary school student*

Waira's First Journey, Eusebio Topooco, author and illustrator, *1987, Bolivia,* HISTORICAL FICTION, *40 pages*

Waira's First Journey is a fascinating, fact-filled book about the Aymara Indians of what is now Bolivia, a people who have existed for more than 25,000 years. It is the story of Waira and her parents as they make a semiannual journey to the market in Topojo. They have brought with them goods to barter and many llamas to carry the supplies they need. Along the way they pass the ruins of the ancient city of Tiwanaku, with its Sun and Moon gates made from huge stone slabs. When they stop at a village near Lake Titicaca, Waira makes a friend and gives him a llama. While sleeping under a starlit sky, Waira's father tells her a story about the totora plant. On every page, Eusebio Topooco's richly colored oil paintings portray aspects of traditional Aymara life. Eusebio Topooco, an Aymaran himself, includes an afterword describing the current conditions of these ancient people.

The Whispering Cloth: A Refugee's Story, Pegi Deitz Shea, illustrated by Anita Riggio, stitched by You Yang, *1995, Thailand,* HISTORICAL FICTION, *30 pages*

Mai lives in the refugee camp in Thailand with her grandma and many other Hmongs from Laos. At the camp, Mai listens to the widows recalling their old life in Laos while they sew *pa'ndau* story cloths to sell to Thai merchants. First, Mai learns to make stitches the size of a grain of rice along the story-cloth borders; by the time the hot season ends, she has become skilled with a needle and thread and wants to make her own *pa'ndau*. Grandma says that Mai has to stitch the story that whispers only to her, and finally in her sleep, "a story was erupting in her head—a story she could stitch." The watercolor illustrations capture the conditions in the camp and the love between a grandmother and granddaughter. Mai's story itself is stitched, and the texture of her *pa'ndau* is palpable. The illustrations, the stitching, and Mai's story together re-create the dreams of a young girl.

> *"Oh dear! Oh dear!"* cried Dorothy, clasping her hands together in dismay; "the house must have fallen on her. What ever shall we do?"
>
> *from The* Wonderful Wizard of Oz *by L. Frank Baum*

The Wizard in the Tree, Lloyd Alexander, illustrated by Laszlo Kubiny, *1975, Europe,* FICTION, *138 pages*

Once long ago, there lived a girl named Mallory who believed in fairy tales—as a young orphan and abused servant, Mallory found in these stories something to hold onto. So when Mallory finds Arbican, an enchanter who has been imprisoned in a tree, she is ecstatic. Arbican, however, is not what Mallory expected. Gruff and grumpy, he scoffs at the myths of wizards—and worst of all, his powers are on the blink, just when Mallory needs them most to help her save her village from the greedy new Squire. Levelheaded Mallory and cantankerous Arbican are destined for many exciting adventures before everything works out in the end. The pace of the novel is fast, and the dialogue between Mallory and Arbican is hilarious.

The Wonderful Wizard of Oz, L. Frank Baum, illustrated by W. W. Denslow, *1900, United States,* FANTASY, *237 pages*

You can always watch the movie, but it's much more fun to read this book aloud and see your children's eyes open wide at descriptions of talking scarecrows, emerald-green cities, melting witches, and fields full of sleep-inducing poppies. The flying monkeys aren't nearly as scary in the book version, although there are a few monsters Hollywood didn't show. All in all, this is a satisfying fantasy story of a little girl who is carried off by a cyclone and deposited in a world wholly unfamiliar to her. Assisted by her little dog, a tin woodman, an animate scarecrow, and a huge lion, young Dorothy embarks on a quest to get back home to Kansas.

The Wreck of the Zanzibar, Michael Morpurgo, illustrated by François Place, *1995, England,* FICTION, *69 pages*

When Great-aunt Laura dies, she leaves behind a diary: "I've lived an ordinary sort of life. But for a few months a long, long time ago, my life was not ordinary at all. This is the diary of those few months." In 1907, Laura's fourteenth year, girls are not allowed to crew the salvage boats that race out from their small island of Scilly to save sailors and collect wreckage from ships that founder in the storms. When the islanders' homes and livelihoods are destroyed by a huge storm, they fear they must all leave for the mainland. Laura cannot bear the thought—but then there is a wreck, and Laura is at the oars of the salvage boat. The wreck and its goods save the islanders and also bring several satisfying and mystifying surprises. There is a simple yet mythical quality to the book; the illustrations— "Laura's" primitive watercolor renderings, and impressionistic watercolors washed with grays, greens, and faint pinks—take the reader to Laura's harsh and lovely world.

Yang the Third and Her Impossible Family, Lensey Namioka, illustrated by Kees de Kiefte, *1995, United States,* FICTION, *143 pages*

Yingmei Yang and her family have recently moved from China to Seattle, and Yingmei—Mary to her American friends—is trying desperately to fit in among her new classmates. To her utter dismay, her family is constantly embarrassing her. Her mother compliments people by telling them they are fat or old, her oldest brother won't play sports and only wants to practice the violin, and her father just can't say his *r*'s correctly. Determined to do it "right," Mary keeps a running list of American sayings and offers to adopt a kitten because it may make popular Holly like her, even though Mary knows her parents would never agree to a cat. In a funny and fast-moving story, Lensey Namioka teaches readers that everybody is different, it's wonderful to love your family, and what's most important is to be yourself.

A Young Painter: The Life and Paintings of Wang Yani—China's Extraordinary Young Artist, Zheng Zhensun and Alice Low, *1991, China,* BIOGRAPHY, *77 pages*

For Wang Yani, painting is a passion. At age four, she began having public showings of her works in China, and in 1989, at the age of fourteen, she became the youngest artist to have a one-person show at the Smithsonian Institution. *A Young Painter* tells her story simply, and is filled with numerous examples of her art. Yani was born in the countryside and many of her early works are of animals, especially monkeys. When she was nine she did a 35-foot-long painting of 112 variously positioned monkeys, each with a different expression. Her paintings now include landscapes, people, and other animals, mixing in fantasy while continuing her use of bold and broad strokes. She has been encouraged by her father, an artist himself, who found ways to challenge her without interfering with her style. Yani also likes to sing and play sports; she does well at school and misses her home when she travels, yet she doesn't come across as the perfect child. She loves painting but she also works hard, and is supported, not spoiled, by strong and loving parents.

MOVING ON
AGE 10 AND UP

These books are more complex in style or content, sometimes both. Thought-provoking, funny, disquieting, or reassuring, they widen a reader's world and sense of identity. Great discussions can happen when a young reader and an adult read these books separately or together, then share their thoughts.

By now, reading may be as integral a part of your life as sleeping, eating, or talking. Books are your retreat on a bad day; they give you wise counsel when you are filled with questions, or a limitless travel itinerary when your boundaries seem too small. They provide a place where you can find assurance, excitement, and inspiration.

Just when you think no one else could possibly understand what you are thinking or feeling, you open a book and—there—you find a friend. Maybe this character lived five hundred years ago, maybe you live in New York City and she lives in a faraway desert, but she understands. Reaching across time and continents, she teaches you to find your similarities and appreciate your differences. It's a skill you can use forever, a gift that books give you.

Agnes de Mille: Dancing Off the Earth, Beverly Gherman, *1990, United States,* BIOGRAPHY, *138 pages*

Agnes de Mille always wanted to dance, but in the early 1900s, dance was not a "respectable" career choice, even though Agnes lived in Hollywood and her uncle was the famous director Cecil B. De Mille. Agnes was thirteen before she could convince her parents she should have dance lessons, and by then it was clear her body would never have the long and willowy lines usually expected of a professional dancer. Agnes stuck with her dream and continued to dance, and after many years of hard work she became a world-famous choreographer, known for her ability to combine ballet with folk traditions from around the world. Drawing heavily on Agnes de Mille's own writing, Beverly Gherman's biography is a lively and fascinating portrait of this determined, talented woman.

> Once in a very rare year, comes along a new book, and I say, as I'm reading, as my eyes eat words without a blink, as my heart and mind grab each other, This, I say, is The Best Book.
>
> Jill Robinson, writer

Alanna: The First Adventure, Tamora Pierce, *1983, Europe,* FANTASY, *241 pages*

The time is long ago. Alanna wants to become a knight; her twin brother Thom wants to be a sorcerer. Easily deceiving their absentminded father, they change places and dress Alanna as a boy so she can go off for Thom's training and Thom can study sorcery. Alanna, now Alan, faces many challenges: she must hide her gender while living with a group of other pages-in-training, and develop her skills at fencing, riding, wrestling, court manners, math, reading, and military history. Small for her ten years, she must practice longer and harder than anyone else, but she is also lucky; befriended by two powerful allies, the king of thieves and the Prince, she learns much and proves her worth. And as time goes on she learns to use her "gift," the magic that will help her save a society. The first in a series, *Alanna: The First Adventure* goes into absorbing detail concerning Alanna's training, the rich atmosphere, and the interesting range of allies and enemies, and presents Alanna as a fiery, resourceful girl.

Among the Volcanoes, Omar S. Castaneda, *1991, Guatemala,* FICTION, *183 pages*

Isabel Pacay lives in a small mountain town in Guatemala. Like most of the girls in her village, she helps with the household chores and is expected to marry young. When her mother becomes seriously ill, everyone assumes Isabel will give up school and stay home. Yet Isabel is different; she wants to pursue her education and become a teacher. As her mother's condition worsens and she refuses the Western medicine that might make her well, Isabel has to fight hard to keep her goals. This is a story about the collision of cultures—of the good and the bad of both sides—and while Omar Castaneda occasionally loses the story in a lecture, he has created a strong female character in Isabel, whose solution for herself requires both courage on her part and change for her boyfriend.

> *Books, books, books. It was not that I read so much. I read and reread the same ones. But all of them were necessary to me. Their presence, their smell, the letters of their titles, and the texture of their leather bindings.*
>
> *Colette, writer*

Anne of Green Gables, L. M. Montgomery, *1908, United States,* FICTION, *308 pages*

Marilla and Mathew expected a boy from the orphanage to help them with farm work. What arrives on the train is Anne, with her red hair, cute nose, and incredible imagination. Anne can make magic, mystery, and romance out of the most mundane situations—and she never seems to stop talking. She is enchanting in her own way, full of quirks and capers, brought up in the school of hard knocks and grateful for love. She is the kind of child who gives every plant an affectionate name, forgets to finish chores because she gets lost in a dream, and will try anything on a dare. Marilla and Mathew end up being captivated by her, as generations of readers have been.

Annie on My Mind, Nancy Garden, *1982, United States,* FICTION, *234 pages*

One day in the Metropolitan Museum of Art, high school senior Liza Winthrop meets Annie Kenyon. Liza attends a small private school with a rigid honor code, while Annie battles her way through a rough public high school across town. Liza loves to hear Annie sing, Annie is fascinated by Liza's architectural drawings, and they both find it more and more important to spend time together. At times each is uncertain how to act upon her feelings, and Liza in particular has difficulty understanding how her love for Annie affects her own identity, yet each knows that nothing has ever made her happier than their relationship. Just when it seems Annie and Liza have found their own way, however, the outside world crashes in. Realistic in its description of the obstacles and discrimination Annie and Liza face, celebratory in the happiness they share, *Annie on My Mind* offers a sympathetic and insightful portrayal of first love.

Back Home, Michelle Magorian, *1984, England,* FICTION, *375 pages*

In 1940, when Virginia was a small and quiet girl of seven, she was evacuated from England to the United States. Now World War II is ending and she has returned, but her mother scarcely recognizes her daughter, now a confident, opinionated twelve-year-old American who calls herself Rusty. In England, Rusty must find her way in a strict and oppressive boarding school filled with malicious girls who despise her for her accent, liberal attitudes, and clothes. For her part, Rusty's mother, who has become a skilled auto mechanic in the last five years, must decide if she will give up the independence she has gained during the war. Rusty's father, steeped in patriarchal attitudes, returns home from his military duties to find that his family falls dramatically short of his expectations. Their predicaments teach us a great deal both about England at the end of World War II and about coming to understand difference while maintaining one's identity. Rusty is blunt, funny, and wonderfully stubborn, and if the eventual resolution is a bit didactic, it's satisfying.

Beauty: A Retelling of the Story of Beauty and the Beast, Robin McKinley, *1978, Europe,* FANTASY, *247 pages*

There are many versions of *Beauty and the Beast*, and while Robin McKinley keeps to the general story line, she also deviates in thought-provoking and interesting ways. In this version, Beauty is the youngest daughter of a prosperous ship merchant who is ruined financially at the beginning of the story. The family moves to the country and begins a simple life in a small house near an enchanted forest. When Father goes on a business trip, Beauty asks only for a single rose when he returns. Following tradition, Beauty is the price of the rose her father picks from the Beast's enchanted garden. But this Beauty is level-headed, persistent, and not ravishingly beautiful, a young woman who learns to look not only beyond appearances but into other worlds and ways of perceiving.

> *Books are meat and / medicine / and flame and flight and /*
> *flower / steel, stitch, cloud and clout, / and drumbeats on the air*
> *Gwendolyn Brooks, poet*

Betsey Brown: A Novel, Ntozake Shange, *1985, United States,* FICTION, *207 pages*

Growing up in St. Louis in the summer of 1959, Betsey Brown is part of a large, proud African-American family. Her father is an energetic, passionate man, a surgeon who wakes the children every morning with bongo drums and a series of questions about African-based history and culture. Her mother is a strikingly beautiful psychiatric social worker who loves her husband and children, yet isn't quite sure how she ended up where she is. Betsey's grandmother keeps the household together and shakes her head over her daughter's dark-skinned husband. The kids run a bit wild. Betsey is starting to notice boys, and the Civil Rights movement is about to have a profound effect on the whole family. Family squabbles, first kisses, a short-lived flight from home, all happen in rich, rapid-fire dialogue that sweeps you along like a great warm river.

A Bone from a Dry Sea, Peter Dickinson, *1992, Africa,* FICTION, *199 pages*

   A Bone from a Dry Sea takes place in two time periods: Now and Then. "Now" is contemporary Africa, where Vinny, determined to establish a relationship with her father, has joined him on a fossil dig. "Then" is prehistoric time, and centers on a girl named Li, who will eventually lead her people in their progress as a species. The story lines mirror each other as Vinny and Li must each face up to aggressive male figures and resolve conflicts between her own ideas and those of the group. As a collection of fossils is found in the Now time, the stories reach across time to merge in an absorbing narrative that raises its own questions about the evolution of humankind.

The Borning Room, Paul Fleischman, *1991, United States,* FICTION, *101 pages*

   In the 1830s, Georgina's grandfather moved to Ohio and built a house with a borning room—a small room off the kitchen where family births and deaths occur. According to Georgina: "It's not a room that's seen much use. But . . . most of my life's turnings have taken place here." It's where Georgina was born on a cold January day in 1851, and where, twelve years later, her grandfather lay on his deathbed; even now she can feel his presence. In this room, a runaway slave helped Georgina's mother give birth, lives were saved by midwives and eggshells, and lives were lost with "modern" medicine. Now, in 1918, Georgina is on the bed in the borning room thinking of her grandson fighting in Europe and her granddaughter tending the wounded there. Looking at the tree her grandfather planted and the flowers her mother nurtured, she wonders about the price of progress and feels grateful that she has always lived in this home.

A Break with Charity: A Story About the Salem Witch Trials, Ann Rinaldi, *1992, United States,* HISTORICAL FICTION, *284 pages*

Ann Rinaldi is a well-known author of historical fiction for young adults, and *A Break with Charity* is one of her most powerful books. It recalls the Salem witch trials of the late seventeenth century from the vantage point of a young woman, Susanna English, who knows that the circle of girls accusing various townspeople of witchcraft are lying, but who is too frightened to tell what she knows. While the book is based on historical events and real people, Ann Rinaldi allows herself the license to elaborate and focus upon Susanna's personal decisions and moral searching in the midst of a town gone hysterical. Part history lesson, part love story, *A Break with Charity* is also a warning, for Ann Rinaldi makes clear that what occurred in Salem could easily happen again under the right conditions.

> *In my English class in seventh grade we practiced speed reading. . . . But it seemed so slow considering all the pages I wanted to read. Wouldn't it be wonderful, I thought, if you could absorb the words through your skin?*
>
> Brooke Abercrombie, *management consultant*

Calico Bush, Rachel Field, woodcuts by Allen Lewis, *1931, United States,* FICTION, *201 pages*

It's unusual to find a book about pioneers in Maine in the eighteenth century, and to discover one that is eminently readable is a real treat. *Calico Bush* focuses on the story of young Marguerite Ledoux—now Maggie—bound out as a servant after she is left without support in the New World. Her French heritage makes her an object of suspicion, but courageous, intelligent Maggie proves invaluable to the Sargent family as they struggle against storms, Maine winters, and Indians. The details have depth and are well-researched, the adventures and challenges are realistic and suspenseful, and the intricate woodcuts scattered throughout the text are a perfect complement.

Cat Running, Zilpha Keatley Snyder, *1994, United States,* FICTION, *168 pages*

Sixth-grader Cat Kinsey is the fastest runner in Brownwood School, until a boy arrives dressed in raggedy overalls and no shoes and shows her up. Zane Perkins is an "Okie," his family dislocated from their farm in Texas by tremendous dust storms. Cat is jealous of his talent and reacts by mirroring her family's distrust and prejudice about Okies. A chance meeting with Zane's little sister, however, begins to open her eyes. Through her relationship with Zane's family and her growing understanding of her own father, Cat learns to overcome her preconceptions in this powerful Depression-era story.

Celebrating the Hero, Lyll Becerra de Jenkins, *1993, Colombia,* FICTION, *179 pages*

When Camila receives an invitation to a ceremony celebrating her deceased grandfather's contributions to a small Colombian town, she feels she must go to represent her mother. She knows her mother would be proud of this honor for him, and since her mother's sudden death ten months ago, "family" has taken on a new importance for Camila. Although her grandfather died before she was born, the stories Mama told made him a hero in Camila's mind. The journey to Colombia takes her farther from her Connecticut home than she could have ever imagined. Through frank writing that handles difficult topics—the abuses of power and its aftermath, how truth can vary with each person—history unfolds for seventeen-year-old Camila. Slowly, she learns painful truths about her grandfather and her mother, and while saddened by her loss, she is also strengthened by the power of forgiveness and the loyalties of families.

Chain of Fire, Beverly Naidoo, illustrated by Eric Velasquez, *1989, South Africa,* FICTION, *242 pages*

One day, fifteen-year-old Naledi returns from collecting water at the town's water tap to find that white numbers have been painted on the door of her home in Bophelong, South Africa. The villagers learn they are to be moved in four weeks' time to Bophutha-tswana—a "homeland" for people who speak Tswana. Those who don't speak Tswana will be moved somewhere else, even if it means separating families. Against seemingly impossible odds, Naledi and other teenagers choose to rebel, as do some of the adults. What happens then provides eye-opening and often disturbing insights into South Africa's not-so-distant history.

> *Books are the carriers of civilization. Without books, history is silent, literature dumb, science crippled, thought and speculation at a standstill. . . . Books are humanity in print.*
> *Barbara W. Tuchman, historian and writer*

Child of the Owl, Laurence Yep, *1977, United States,* FICTION, *215 pages*

Cassie's father is a gambler, and this time he's in more trouble than usual. As a result, Cassie ends up staying with her maternal grandmother in a tiny apartment in San Francisco's Chinatown. For independent, levelheaded, slightly defensive Cassie, this is her first real encounter with her grandmother and an initiation into her Chinese heritage. There's plenty of plot to this novel, but more important are the well-drawn and sometimes eccentric characters, the developing relationship between Cassie and her equally independent grandmother, and the part played by Chinatown itself. Laurence Yep makes 1950s Chinatown a living, breathing place as he delves into the heart and soul of what it means to be Chinese, American, and part of a family.

Children of the River, Linda Crew, *1989, United States and Cambodia,* FICTION, *213 pages*

The Cambodian refugees who worked on Linda Crew's farm in Corvallis, Oregon, inspired her to write this moving book about a teenager named Sundara, who escapes with her aunt's family when the Khmer Rouge army sweeps through Cambodia. Left behind are Sundara's parents and little sister, their fate unknown. In the United States, Sundara must negotiate her way between the rigid expectations and rules of her aunt, who expects Sundara to follow Cambodian traditions, and the looser social customs of her new country. When a handsome schoolmate named Jonathon McKinnon shows a marked interest in her, Sundara must decide which traditions make sense for her, even if it means risking her aunt's anger. Made stronger by her experiences, Sundara is becoming a principled, intelligent, and thoughtful young woman, determined to overcome all obstacles on her way to becoming a doctor and loving Jonathon.

> *A book is the only place in which you can examine a fragile thought without breaking it, or explore an explosive idea without fear it will go off in your face. It is one of the few havens remaining where [your] mind can get both provocation and privacy.*
>
> Edward P. Morgan, *writer*

Daphne's Book, Mary Downing Hahn, *1983, United States,* FICTION, *177 pages*

Jessica is in middle school, wears glasses, and likes to read; she has friends, but she knows she is not part of the popular crowd. In her English class, the teacher pairs her with Daphne, a strange new girl at school, and assigns them to write a children's book. The teacher explains to an unhappy Jessica that she is the best writer and Daphne is the best artist, and together they should write a wonderful book. Forced to spend time with Daphne, Jessica gets to know a strong, talented girl who is dealing with situations beyond her control, secrets Jessica promises not to tell. Jessica struggles with the problem of liking Daphne and being ridiculed at school by those who don't; she fails herself a few times as she learns what it means to be a friend.

The reader may find herself both disappointed in and exhilarated with Jessica as she faces conflicts in this absorbing novel.

Deliver Us from Evie, M. E. Kerr, *1994, United States,* FICTION, *177 pages*

At eighteen, Evie is one of the hardest workers on her family farm in Missouri. Whenever the farm equipment or cars need repairs, it's Evie who does them. Her mother says that Evie is just like her dad: "She listened to him, walked like him, talked like him, told jokes just like him." *Deliver Us from Evie* is narrated by Evie's younger brother Doug, and through him we see a broad picture of a small Midwestern community. Eventually, Evie's sexual preference can no longer be ignored by her family, especially in light of her relationship with the banker's daughter. It's difficult for her mother not to believe that if Evie just wore different clothes, had another haircut, or showed some interest in Cord Whittle, that her life would be better. But Evie remains true to herself and Doug realizes that "she was deep-down different." Told with compassion, humor, and strong character development, *Deliver Us from Evie* is about first romances for both Evie and Doug, and the strength of family love.

The Devil's Arithmetic, Jane Yolen, *1988, Poland,* FICTION, *170 pages*

Twelve-year-old Hannah doesn't want to be at her grandparents' house for Passover Seder dinner. She thinks the traditions are boring, as is Grandfather Will, who always brings up the Holocaust. But when Hannah is asked to open the door for the prophet Elijah, she opens the door to another time. In this new place, she is Chaya, taken along with the rest of the villagers to a concentration camp. Jane Yolen's powerful story follows Hannah's evolution from contemporary teenager to someone who experiences the full horror of the Holocaust. As her understanding grows, the tension of the story deepens. It would be impossible for this book not to contain graphic, heartrending violence, but the messages it conveys about remembering humanity, about courage and cruelty and sacrifice, are important and well portrayed.

Dicey's Song, Cynthia Voigt, *1982, United States,* FICTION, *211 pages*

"The Tillermans traveled on a road, and roads ended . . . [their] road had rolled up against Gram's house, and they had tumbled off it into Gram's—Dicey grinned. Not exactly into Gram's arms, maybe not into her lap. Certainly into her life." It was a long summer for Dicey, traveling down the East Coast with her three younger siblings, trying to reach Gram's house after Mom left them. Now, with Gram, in her ramshackle house on the beach, they have a chance to be a family. It's not easy. Gram is gruff and has a reputation among the townspeople as an eccentric. Little Maybeth is a musical genius but slow in school. Sammy needs to fight; James just wants to have friends. And Dicey? At thirteen, too old for her years, she has to learn to grow up and grow young at the same time in this beautiful, painful, extraordinary book.

> *I put the tools back in my pocket and ran all the way back to town, jumping over all the obstacles in my way, sliding, falling, picking myself up, and running until I reached the house. I threw the door to the shop open and tore up the stairs yelling "Mama! Mama! I found it."*
>
> *from* The Dragon in the Cliff *by Sheila Cole*

The Dragon in the Cliff: A Novel Based on the Life of Mary Anning, Sheila Cole, illustrated by T. C. Farrow, *1991, England,* BIOGRAPHICAL FICTION, *211 pages*

In 1811, thirteen-year-old Mary Anning discovered the first complete Ichthyosaur skeleton. Mary had been hunting fossils since she was seven, when her father began taking her along as he looked for the "curiosities" he sold to rich vacationers who came to their beach town of Lyme. Mary became hooked on fossils and remained a fossil hunter throughout her life. A working-class woman, she was never accepted into the scientific societies whose members created theories from evidence, yet her discoveries were crucial to those theories. Sheila Cole spent several years researching the material for *The*

Dragon in the Cliff. Her historical novel re-creates Mary's intense curiosity and determination, and explores the precarious social position she was placed in by her "unfeminine" work.

Dragonsong, Anne McCaffrey, *1985, Other Worlds,* FANTASY, *202 pages*
    Menolly is a multitalented girl—she plays music like a Masterharper and can run faster than most of the boys. On the planet of Pern, in a community where people live in fear of the deadly Threadfall that comes from a passing red star, girls are not supposed to be musicians. So Menolly's father, the leader of the community, makes sure that the old Masterharper's replacement knows nothing of Menolly's musical ability. Denied her gift and identity, Menolly runs away, straight into danger and wonder. Menolly's dilemma and frustration are familiar, but the context—an otherworldly setting complete with flying dragons, fire lizards, unusual plants, and a place called "between"—is fantastic and imaginative. Of course Menolly's talent wins out in the end, but the journey to recognition and success is far more exciting when you spend it in the company of many-colored fire lizards with whirling eyes and delightful personalities.

Drifting Snow: An Arctic Journey, James Houston, author and illustrator, *1992, Canada,* HISTORICAL FICTION, *150 pages*
    When Elizabeth Queen was a toddler, the government took her away from her Inuk family because of a tuberculosis outbreak, and then lost her identity papers. Now near the age of thirteen, Elizabeth is trying to find her home. Although this island village of eighteen people is not her family, the villagers invite her to stay with them and learn Inuk language and ways, including their deep respect for nature's abundance and power. Elizabeth learns her own lesson within weeks of her arrival. While she is under the ice walking along the ocean floor picking up clams, the ice starts to break up over her head and the entire village rescues her and two others from certain death. Later at their summer camp, Elizabeth works alongside the villagers as they fish and hunt with other Inuits. The trip back to their winter camp, complete with a broken canoe, ice floes, and seals, will have readers on the edge of their seats. James Houston draws on his own

experiences in the Arctic to capture the harshness of conditions, the Inuks' love of family and nature, and the thrill and confusion Elizabeth feels through it all.

> *I open a book to move into another world. Nothing thrills me quite as much as seeing how certain words, put together in a certain way, are capable of creating a world I can return to whenever I wish.*
>
> Hilary Horder Hippeley, *writer*

Earthquake at Dawn, Kristiana Gregory, *1992, United States,* HISTORICAL FICTION, *188 pages*

On April 18, 1906, San Francisco was devastated by an 8.3 earthquake. When the earthquake struck, Edith Irvine, photographer and 22-year-old daughter of the prosperous Irvine family, was on board a boat in the San Francisco harbor. After she disembarked, she hid her camera equipment in a baby buggy to avoid police and soldiers who would have stopped her, and took some of the only pictures of the destruction. Kristiana Gregory tells strong-willed Edith's story through the eyes of a fictional character, Edith's 15-year-old companion, Daisy Valentine. Embellished with actual photographs and excerpts from letters, *Earthquake at Dawn* is an effective history lesson and a portrait of an exceptional woman.

Eleanor Roosevelt: A Life of Discovery, Russell Freedman, *1993, United States,* BIOGRAPHY, *191 pages*

Eleanor Roosevelt truly was a citizen of the world, and Russell Freedman's candid and informative biography of her is a pleasure to read. Born in 1884, Eleanor was a shy, quiet child who had a serious nature and a keen awareness of others. She married her distant cousin Franklin Roosevelt in 1905; they had six children in ten years, and many expected Eleanor to settle into the role of wife and mother. But during World War I she was a Red Cross volunteer, and in 1920 she joined the newly formed League of Women Voters. After her husband was stricken with polio in 1921, Eleanor became his confidante, affecting his views of the country and the world, and was a great ally in his political career until his death in 1945. After FDR's death she was appointed a delegate to the United Nations, served as a goodwill ambassador for the United States, and traveled widely as a private citizen. Near the end of her life she wrote: "It was not until I reached middle age that I had the courage to develop interests of my own. . . . I long ago reached the point where there is no living person I fear, and few challenges that I am not willing to face."

The Eternal Spring of Mr. Ito, Sheila Garrigue, *1985, Canada,* FICTION, *163 pages*

Sara has been sent from England to stay with her aunt and uncle in Vancouver, British Columbia, to be farther away from the fighting of World War II. But when the Japanese bomb Pearl Harbor, the war comes to Sara. Sara's cousin's fiancé is killed, and Sara's Uncle Duncan immediately and angrily fires Mr. Ito, his longtime Japanese friend and gardener. Almost overnight, Japanese-Canadians are suspect; soon they are rounded up and sent to internment camps. Sara struggles to comprehend the hatred and to save the precious bonsai tree that Mr. Ito helped her plant. When she accidentally finds Mr. Ito hidden in a seaside cave, preparing for a death he prefers over dishonor, his wisdom helps her in her commitment to do the right thing and refuse to accept prejudice, regardless of the risks.

Fat Chance, Lesléa Newman, *1994, United States,* FICTION, *214 pages*

The start of a new school year is a chance for thirteen-year-old Judi Beth Liebowitz to set some goals. She wants to figure out what she'll be when she grows up, find a boyfriend, and lose some weight—in fact, she'll start her diet tomorrow. Her English teacher assigns everyone to keep a diary, and Judi's story is told through her entries. Faithfully, Judi writes in her diary, revealing her innermost thoughts about her friends, body image, and home life. It is soon apparent that Judi is obsessed with weight, hers and others'. A chance encounter with a popular, skinny girl at school begins a path of bingeing and purging for Judi. Lesléa Newman provides sympathetic insight into an issue many find incomprehensible, though she offers no easy solutions. Readers may finish this book with sad hearts, but also with knowledge that may help them and/or their friends.

> *"I don't know," [Elizabeth] said, "what I'm going to be." She put out her lower lip thoughtfully, and as usual took time making up her mind. "But I think," she said, and her expression was serious, "that it will be something hard."*
>
> *from* The First Woman Doctor *by Rachel Baker*

The First Woman Doctor: The Story of Elizabeth Blackwell, M.D., Rachel Baker, illustrated by Corinne Malvern, *1944, United States,* BIOGRAPHY, *246 pages*

Raised by parents who believed in equal education for their daughters and sons, Elizabeth Blackwell chose medicine as her goal. She encountered formidable obstacles; in the 1840s, no woman in the United States had ever even applied to medical school. After being rejected by numerous institutions, she was accepted into Geneva College as part of a prank. Undaunted when she discovered the truth, she went on to prove herself admirably. Zealous in her search for challenges, she let nothing stand in her way. Although an accident took most of her eyesight early in her career and she had to give up her dream of becoming a surgeon, she went on to open the first school of nursing in the United States, the New York Infirmary College to train women doctors, and the National Health Society in England to teach hygiene and disease prevention. The epitome of grit and unwavering resolve, she is an extraordinary role model.

The Fledgling, Jane Langton, *1980, United States,* FANTASY, *182 pages*

Eight-year-old Georgie, light as a puff of dandelion seeds, isn't sure if she can fly or not. She had a dream—or was it reality? She tries leaping down the hall stairs and falls hard; jumping off the front porch, for a moment it feels as if she soars. Then a huge Canadian goose arrives with the southern migration, landing in Walden Pond near her house, and soon Georgie is flying nightly with him, first on his back, then drifting down on currents of air in a long, graceful descent to the ground. But Mr. Preek, the uptight banker, and his assistant, the nervous and zealously organized Miss Prawn, are upset by anything out of the ordinary, and there is definitely something not normal about Georgie. And that goose—why, nearsighted Mr. Preek thought he saw it attacking the little girl one day. So now he has a gun and is just waiting for the full moon and the start of hunting season. Exhilarating as a flying dream, this is a marvelous, quirky tale of good and evil, magic and belief.

> *Most of us live in two worlds—our real world and the one we build or spin for ourselves out of the books we read, the heroes we admire, the things we hope to do.*
>
> from Fog Magic *by Julia L. Sauer*

Fog Magic, Julia L. Sauer, *1943, Canada,* FANTASY, *107 pages*

For most people in Greta's Nova Scotia fishing village, fog is a source of fear or frustration. But in every generation of Addingtons, there has been a child who loves the fog, and Greta is one of them. The year she is eleven, she goes exploring when the fog is thick and sees the outlines of buildings where there should only be the sunken cellar holes of a long-deserted fishing town called Blue Cove. For the next year, every time the conditions are right, Greta visits Blue Cove. There she meets people who died long ago, people with hopes, mysteries, and stories of their own. Real to the touch when the fog is thick, they and their town disappear when the sun breaks through. In that year before she turns twelve and loses Blue Cove once and for all, she learns from these villagers lessons both simple and profound in this wise, eloquent book.

For the Life of Laetitia, Merle Hodge, *1993, Trinidad,* FICTION, *224 pages*

Laetitia is the first of her family to be picked to go to the secondary school in La Puerta, the nearby town, and everyone is proud of her. Her father, who lives in the town and whom she has hardly ever seen, has even promised to pay her fees and let her live with him and his wife. It is a big opportunity, but it isn't easy. Laetitia's father can be a tyrant, and her teachers at school tend to be racist and elitist. It is hard to learn when you are homesick for your family and the smells, sights, and warmth of your home. Merle Hodge makes Laetitia a real human being—confused, determined, angry, and loving—as she tries to gain an education in the midst of conflicting expectations and traditions.

> *It was natural as a girl to see myself more as Maid Marian; and I sometimes found that rather irritating. Marian was usually locked up in a castle and needing to be rescued—being terribly brave about it, of course. What I really wanted was to imagine myself running through the forest, along with the men. I wanted to be the one doing the rescuing.*
>
> *from the afterword to* The Forestwife *by Theresa Tomlinson*

The Forestwife, Theresa Tomlinson, *1993, England,* FICTION, *166 pages*

When Mary learns she is to wed an elderly widower with rotten teeth, she flees her uncle's manor and hides in the forest with the help of her childhood nurse, Agnes. In the forest, Agnes becomes the Forestwife, a healer the local people turn to in their time of trouble. Agnes is kept busy, for there is much trouble: the lords are greedy and the monarchy unsettled. In the forest, Mary matures and becomes Marian, a strong and compassionate woman, and eventually the Forestwife. Full of the details of everyday life in medieval times and carried by a strong story line, *The Forestwife* portrays a three-dimensional Maid Marian in a book that is almost impossible to put down.

From the Mixed-Up Files of Mrs. Basil E. Frankweiler, E. L. Konigsburg, *1967, United States,* FICTION, *176 pages*

Claudia is tired of living at home, "bored with simply being straight-A Claudia Kincaid." So, taking her little brother James with her (he's the sibling with the most money and the ability to keep his mouth shut), she sets off to hide in the Metropolitan Museum of Art in New York City. For a week they escape detection, take baths in the restaurant fountain, and sleep in elegant, ancient beds. E. L. Konigsburg captures the excitement, the suspense, the thrill, and the imagination involved in such an adventure; you'll never look at a museum the same way again. Eventually, Claudia and James become fascinated by a beautiful statue and the mystery that surrounds it. Solving the mystery takes them to new places, new people, and, for Claudia, a new sense of herself. A great solo read, this book also serves well as a read-aloud for younger children.

Go Ask Alice, Anonymous, *1967, United States,* JOURNAL, *188 pages*

Go Ask Alice is the real diary of a fifteen-year-old middle-class white girl who takes her first drug trip unknowingly, and then, spurred on by loneliness and a lack of self-confidence, continues to seek out new drugs. Within an astonishingly short period of time, she has become a dealer, then a runaway. Her longing to return to her family and her normal life is heartbreaking, particularly when her attempts are undermined by frustrated former "friends." In the end, she does not succeed. *Go Ask Alice* is a frightening book, but it is important reading for both adolescents and their parents. Alice never thought of herself as someone who would take drugs, and her motivations may be unsettlingly familiar to many readers, even thirty years later.

Grace, Jill Paton Walsh, *1991, England,* BIOGRAPHICAL FICTION, *253 pages*

One night in 1838, Grace Darling spotted a shipwreck from her father's lighthouse on the Northumbrian coast. She and her father took out a boat and rescued nine survivors. Because she was female, Grace became a public phenomenon—unwanted gifts, money, and letters poured in; the townspeople became jealous; and Grace's life was changed forever. Working with primary material, excerpting from letters and newspaper accounts, Jill Walsh re-creates Grace Darling, her brave act, and all that followed. The language is beautiful, if sometimes challenging; the issues of courage, fame, and greed, as well as the wrestling of Grace's conscience, take this well beyond a straightforward story of heroism.

> *Be you writer or reader, it is very pleasant to run away in a book.*
>
> *Jean Craighead George, writer*

Harriet the Spy, Louise Fitzhugh, *1964, United States,* FICTION, *240 pages*

Perhaps it's because of all Harriet gets away with, or her self-confidence, or her painfully honest note taking that lands her in a lot of trouble, but *Harriet the Spy* has been a favorite with readers for more than thirty years. At age eleven, Harriet already has a regular spy route through her neighborhood, and she's never without her special spy equipment—including flashlight, canteen, extra pens, a pocket knife, and her most important item, her notebook full of observations. For Harriet, nothing is sacred as she comments freely on the private lives of her schoolmates and the people with whom she comes into casual contact. One day at school, however, her classmates get hold of the notebook, and after that, nothing is the same. Yet even in a fix, Harriet comes up with her own peculiar and humorous take on the situation. Her fans can continue to follow her escapades in *The Long Secret*.

Harriet Tubman: Conductor on the Underground Railroad, Ann Petry, *1955, United States,* BIOGRAPHY, *221 pages*

Harriet Tubman has become an icon of African-American resistance to slavery and prejudice. Ann Petry takes us deep into her life to make us understand her as an ordinary and exceptional human being. When she was a young woman, Harriet preferred working outdoors in the woods; there she became strong and learned to walk without sound. Scarred and handicapped for life by a blow to the head which caused her to "fall asleep" for indefinite periods of time without warning, she was not a natural choice to brave the dangers of the Underground Railroad. Yet she did countless times, and brought more than three hundred slaves to freedom. When the Civil War began, she served as a nurse and a spy. This well-written biography shows her for the remarkable woman she was.

> *I haven't been to Switzerland yet, but when I go, I'll recognize it, all right. I've walked up and down the mountain paths with Heidi; I've seen those meadows of wildflowers.*
>
> *Jean Fritz, writer*

Heidi, Johanna Spyri, illustrated by Cecil Leslie, *1880, Switzerland,* FICTION, *238 pages*

Heidi has been a favorite since it was first published in 1880. Its heroine has good old-fashioned pluck, her reclusive grandfather is an endearingly terrifying combination of outward gruffness and a soft heart, and her friend Peter makes a spirited companion with whom to explore the Swiss Alps. The Alps themselves are an awe-inspiring backdrop for Heidi's growth from an intrepid five-year-old to a thoughtful and loving child, while a stay in the city with an invalid girl develops Heidi's courage and sensitivity. Although the length and the eloquent, detailed descriptions of the original version place *Heidi* at an older reader level, it is a delightful book to read aloud to younger children.

Hero of Lesser Causes, Julie Johnston, *1992, Canada,* FICTION, *194 pages*

Keely loves her older brother Patrick—he's the best person for dare and double-dare, and it's a popular game between them. After Patrick is paralyzed with polio, they no longer play. Vibrant, spunky Keely doesn't know this brother who closes his eyes to the whole world, and she is confused by the changes in her household. She wants to rescue Patrick from himself; she wants to ride horses and be a grown-up. When Keely tells her friend Ginny that she wants to be a hero, Ginny corrects her—"heroine." Keely answers: "Nope, I'd rather be a hero. A mature, womanly hero, just going about my business getting everything fixed up. Oh, I've left childhood behind, Ginny. What you're looking at is a woman." It's a tough year for Keely, trying to grow up at twelve, saving her allowance to buy a horse, living in a house with a brother she can't seem to reach. With the aid of her family, Patrick's nurse, and her own determination, Keely realizes some of her wants, and is on her way to becoming a remarkable, vulnerable, lovable young woman.

Hispanic, Female and Young, Phyllis Tashlik, editor, *1994, United States,* ANTHOLOGY, *217 pages*

In 1987, Phyllis Tashlik, with twelve eighth-grade girls, began a class in the New York public school system called "Las Mujeres Hispanas." It was a course designed to find and read writings by Hispanic women, and to encourage the girls to explore themselves through their own writing. *Hispanic, Female and Young* is a result of their hard work. By combining works of published authors and poets with writings from the class, they explore whole worlds. Chapter headings include "Remembering Our Culture," "La Familia," "El Barrio," and "Prejudice." Poetry celebrates sunrises, grandmothers, and births, and mourns first loves, innocence lost, and island life. Many of the writings are autobiographical and describe life in Mexico, Colombia, Puerto Rico, and Cuba. There are narratives about gender roles, babies having babies, and the importance of dreams and self-direction. This celebration of the written word and cultural identity inspires well beyond the original classroom, through voices that sing, alone and in harmony, of the joys and pains of life.

The Holocaust Lady, Ruth Minsky Sender, *1992, United States,* MEMOIR, *192 pages*

This is a book about learning to speak out, about the importance of memory, family, and religion, and about the hundreds of ways the

Holocaust impacts the daily lives of survivors many years later. Ruth Minsky Sender is the author of *The Cage* and *To Life*, powerful memoirs of her experiences during the Holocaust and her years as a displaced person in Europe. *The Holocaust Lady* describes her immigration to the United States, her joy in creating her own family, and the struggle of living in a country where people were often ignorant of or willing to forget the pain and loss she and other survivors had endured. She describes how, after many years, she decides that their story must be told. When *The Cage* is published, she finds herself being asked to speak at schools and soon has another identity as "The Holocaust Lady," a difficult but rewarding role that she writes about movingly and with great honesty.

> *And how I felt it beat / Under my pillow, in the morning's dark, / An hour before the sun would let me read! / My books!*
> *Elizabeth Barrett Browning, poet*

Homesick: My Own Story, Jean Fritz, illustrated by Margot Tomes, *1982, China and United States,* AUTOBIOGRAPHICAL FICTION, *163 pages*
When Jean Fritz began to write *Homesick*, her memories came out in lumps, not in chronological sequence, so although the events in this book actually happened, she considers it a fictionalized account. Her parents worked in China from 1913 to 1927; Jean was born there in 1915, and *Homesick* covers her life from 1925 to 1927. At age ten, Jean knows she is an American, but having never been to America, she's not quite sure what that means. While her grandmother writes of the chicks hatching on her Pennsylvania farm, Jean, who lives along the Yangtse River, writes about the magician who swallows three yards of fire. She recalls Lin Nai-Nai, her nanny who has been disowned by her family after she left her husband when he took a second wife, and Yang Sze-Fu, the cook who has a fingernail two inches long. There are British and American friends, and in the background, an impending war which eventually becomes the reason

for her family's departure. Spunky, rambunctious Jean finally arrives in the United States, ready for new explorations.

I Am Regina, Sally M. Keehn, *1991, United States,* BIOGRAPHICAL FICTION, *237 pages*
     I Am Regina is a fictionalized retelling of the story of Regina Leininger, captured by Indians from her family's farm in Pennsylvania in 1755. Ten-year-old Regina watches as her father and brother are killed and their farm is burned; then she and her older sister are taken captive. Separated from her sister and forced to carry another young girl, Regina has to walk long days with little food or water until she reaches her new home. "Home" is a hut, where her father's scalp hangs from a pole and where she is beaten for speaking English. Yet gradually, the Indian village does become home, as Regina first finds sympathetic hearts, then learns to understand the Indians' hatred of whites. This is a violent but highly educational book, willing to depict the brutality of both races and the complexity of living on both sides.

Invincible Louisa, Cornelia Meigs, *1933, United States,* BIOGRAPHY, *185 pages*
     A warmly told story of a close-knit family, *Little Women* was based on Louisa May Alcott's memories of her childhood in the mid-nineteenth century. But Louisa's own life was actually far more dramatic. As the daughter of Bronson Alcott—a philosophical visionary whose utopian ideas often placed his family in financial jeopardy—Louisa changed residences constantly throughout her growing-up years. One communal experiment, Fruitlands, almost tore the family apart. When she grew up, Louisa's writing was as much a search for desperately needed financial security for her family as it was for the love of literature. Yet her childhood was rich, her home, loving; family friends included Emerson, Thoreau, and Hawthorne. Nothing made Louisa happier than when her success meant stability and comfort for those she cared for. Cornelia Meigs's biography gives us an evenhanded portrait of Louisa's family and life, with a feisty, determined Louisa at its center.

Island of the Blue Dolphins, Scott O'Dell, *1960, United States,* BIO-
GRAPHICAL FICTION, *181 pages*

Island of the Blue Dolphins was inspired by accounts of the Lost
Woman of San Nicolas, who survived alone on an island off the
Southern California coast from 1835 to 1853. When she was discovered, she could speak only in signs and in her own, strange language,
so little is known of her life. From this mystery Scott O'Dell creates
a fascinating and enthralling tale. When their tribe must leave their
island, twelve-year-old Karana's brother is left behind by mistake.
Karana sees him on the cliffs and leaps from the boat, confident that
their tribe will return for them. Eventually, she realizes she was
wrong, and after her brother is killed by wild dogs, she must learn to
cope with both the physical and emotional challenges she faces. She
breaks a taboo against women using weapons and learns to catch her
own food, makes her own clothing and fortified shelter, and befriends various animals to counteract her deep loneliness. Her
growth is profound, compelling, and lyrically described by one of the
foremost authors of historical fiction for young adults.

> *What I remember most clearly is that I would enter into a sort
> of trance while reading. My mother would often have to come
> and literally pull the book down from my field of view in order
> to get my attention.*
>
> *Cynthia Mayer Seely, writer and researcher*

Journey of the Sparrows, Fran Leeper Buss and Daisy Cubas, *1991, El
Salvador and United States,* FICTION, *155 pages*

What a sad, beautiful, frightening, and hopeful book this is.
Fifteen-year-old Maria and what is left of her family have fled El
Salvador, where the Guardias killed Maria's father for bringing a
teacher to their village. Now Maria, her pregnant sister Julia, and
her little brother Oscar, in nailed-shut crates, are trying to cross the
Mexican-U.S. border. Life in Chicago, when they get there, is hard,
and their mother and baby sister Teresa are still in Mexico. Food and

work are scarce; it is Maria's artwork that finally provides hope. When Mama is caught in Mexico and sent back to El Salvador, most likely to be killed, it is Maria who must go get baby Teresa before she dies. This is a graphic and heart-wrenching book, but it also depicts the strength and beauty in memories and family ties, and compassion among strangers.

Justice and Her Brothers, Virginia Hamilton, *1978, United States,* FAN-TASY, *282 pages*

"Justice is as Justice does"—it's a saying that eleven-year-old Justice repeats often to herself, and it bolsters her confidence. But this summer, her nerves are raw. With Dad working and Mom at school all day, the family house seems to lie in the baking sun, waiting. Waiting for rain, waiting for something to explode. Justice watches her twin thirteen-year-old brothers, Thomas and Levi. They have always seemed to communicate without speaking, but more often now Justice can see Thomas in Levi's face, and it scares her. She knows there is something evil about Thomas; she fears the barely restrained rage that pulsates through his incessant drumming. What Justice does not know yet is her own psychic ability. By the end of the book, she learns to acknowledge and use her power, setting the stage for Virginia Hamilton's *The Justice Cycle,* a series of books, including *Dustland* and *The Gathering,* that propel these players into strange and distant futures.

Karen, Marie Killilea, *1952, United States,* BIOGRAPHY, *286 pages*

When Marie Killilea's daughter Karen was born in 1940, she weighed less than two pounds. She survived, but over time it became apparent she had cerebral palsy. In the 1940s, very little was known about CP; the Killileas visited doctor after doctor, only to be told that Karen had no hope. One doctor dryly commented: "In China, they take such children up on top of a mountain and leave them." The Killileas never gave up. They went into debt, turned their living room into a rehabilitation center, and pulled their family into a close-knit and constantly giving unit, sustained by love and religious faith. Marie Killilea describes both the hardships and the incredible rewards of their life with strong, resourceful, and good-humored Karen as she learns to talk, walk, read, and write.

> *It always amazed me that I could go into the bookstore and for the price of a single meal, buy a story from another world that someone spent years writing . . . small enough to fit into my purse and have it fill me, nourish me in greater ways than food ever could.*
>
> *Gloria Bauermeister, songwriter*

Kiss the Dust, Elizabeth Laird, *1991, Iraq,* HISTORICAL FICTION, *279 pages*

Twelve-year-old Tara Hawrami is aware of the war between Iraq and Iran, and of the Iraqi government's discrimination against its Kurdish citizens, which includes her family, but her own life has remained mostly untouched. But none of the Kurds is above suspicion, and over the course of a few days, sensing that the government is watching them, her family realizes they must flee. So begins a nearly two-year journey that tests Tara's family physically, spiritually, financially, and emotionally. Tara's brother joins the Kurdish freedom fighters, leaving an ache in their hearts. After surviving bombing attacks, they cross the mountainous border between Iraq and Iran under the cover of night. Tara confronts her mother's illness, her once decisive father's helplessness, and her own feelings of terror caused by life in the refugee camps. Portrayed in a narrative that is crisp in detail and historical content, Tara comes to a new understanding of the impact of war, the importance of home—wherever it may be—and the meaning of heritage, for herself and her family.

Laurie Tells, Linda Lowery, illustrated by John Eric Karpinski, *1994, United States,* FICTION, *40 pages*

Eleven-year-old Laurie has been molested by her father for the past two years; it happened again last night. She tried to tell her mom when she was ten, but her mother told her not to let her imagination carry her away. Laurie now finds herself thinking again of people to tell and dismissing them one by one, yet she has to confide in someone. Aunt Jan is the one person Laurie believes can help her, and help her she does. Laurie's pain is palpable in the narrative verse, and as Laurie works through her feelings of betrayed trust and raw emotion, her sense of self grows along with her image in the book's stunning illustrations. *Laurie Tells* empowers the victim, and affords adults a gentle and realistic approach to a very difficult topic.

Letters from a Slave Girl: The Story of Harriet Jacobs, Mary E. Lyons, *1992, United States,* BIOGRAPHICAL FICTION, *137 pages*

Harriet Jacobs's powerful autobiography, *Incidents in the Life of a Slave Girl*, originally published in 1861, was one of the first narratives to describe the pain of slavery from a woman's point of view. In *Letters from a Slave Girl*, Mary Lyons re-creates Harriet Jacobs's life through a series of fictional letters written by Harriet. They tell a story of betrayal—of owners who do not keep promises of freedom, of a master who wants sexual relations with Harriet. In desperation, Harriet runs away and hides in a three-foot-tall, uninsulated garret in her grandmother's house. It is seven years before she is able to leave the garret and flee to the North. Mary Lyons's text is simpler than Harriet Jacobs's version, but the issues of brutality, resistance, and persecution come through clear and strong.

Letters from Rifka, Karen Hesse, *1992, Russia and United States,* FICTION, *148 pages*

Letters from Rifka is based on the experiences of Karen Hesse's great-aunt Lucy Evrutin, whose family fled Russia in the early twentieth century to escape persecution of the Jews. The story is told through a series of letters from twelve-year-old Rifka to her cousin Tovah, written in tiny, tiny script along the margins of a book by Pushkin. Rifka's family finally makes it to Poland, but there they learn that Rifka, who has contracted ringworm, will not be allowed to emigrate until she is healed. The rest of the family must go on. Many months, lessons, and languages later, Rifka reaches Ellis Island, only to be detained once more—she is now bald, and officials say a bald woman has little chance of getting a husband and thus may be a burden to the state. In a triumphant scene, Rifka convinces them otherwise. Rifka's insights, maturity, and curiosity make her a memorable character; her story portrays both horrible injustices and the remarkable courage and caring of individuals.

> It is . . . when / we gloriously forget ourselves, and plunge / soul-forward, headlong, into a book's profound, / Impassioned for its beauty, and salt of truth— / 'Tis then we get the right good from a book.
>
> *Elizabeth Barrett Browning, poet*

The Little White Horse, Elizabeth Goudge, *1946, England,* FANTASY, *277 pages*

Young Maria Merryweather has quite a task before her when she arrives at her uncle's palatial English estate. There must be magic here—how else to explain a cat that can write hieroglyphics, a dog that looks a bit too much like a lion, and the evil that seems to lurk in the forest beyond? On top of all that, it appears that it is up to her to right the wrongs of past generations and bring peace and prosperity to the estate and the town that lies nearby. It will take all of her courage, intelligence, and patience (something she has little of) to make everyone live happily ever after. *The Little White Horse* provides a great escape; the descriptions are dense and lush, the flights of imagination tickle your thoughts, and the eventual resolution of good over evil is both exciting and satisfying.

Lupita Mañana, Patricia Beatty, *1981, United States,* FICTION, *186 pages*

When thirteen-year-old Lupita's father is swept overboard from a fishing boat and drowned, it is up to Lupita and her older brother Salvador to cross the border between Mexico and the United States in search of work that can support their family. Tijuana and the illegal border crossing are a nightmare, but life in the United States holds even more pain and fear. Work, when they find it, is hard; La Migra and deportation are a constant danger; and Salvador soon becomes more interested in clothes and motorcycles than in sending money home to Mama. Wise, strong, but still an adolescent, Lupita perseveres. *Lupita Mañana* is a sympathetic and thought-provoking exploration of the issues of illegal immigration.

Make Lemonade, Virginia Euwer Wolff, *1993, United States,* FICTION, *200 pages*

"I'm standing in their smelly apartment / looking over the way things are going to be, / me with these two small ones that I can already tell / are leaking liquids everywhere." Writing in verse form, fourteen-year-old LaVaughn describes her experiences as she works for and eventually befriends Jolly, a seventeen-year-old mother who is in desperate need of a friend. But LaVaughn's plans for college—her reason for taking this baby-sitting job—are not part of Jolly's world; Jolly never finished high school and is now a single mother with two children. With unique free verse and a stream-of-conscious style, *Make Lemonade* is a realistic portrayal of these young women's lives and hopes, and how they can and can't help each other.

Margaret Mead, Julie Castiglia, *1989, United States,* BIOGRAPHY, *125 pages*

Born in 1901, Margaret Mead grew up in a house full of strong and diverse people whose philosophies reverberated throughout her long, fascinating life. Her mother imparted a concern and awareness of the whole world; her father emphasized listening and knowing all the facts. From her grandmother, who taught her at home during some of her early school years, came a sense of fairness and trust. In 1924, at the age of twenty-three, Margaret said good-bye to her husband and family and sailed to Samoa to conduct an anthropological study of young women there. Out of this research came *Coming of Age in Samoa,* the first of her many books. Throughout her life she traveled extensively in remote areas of the world, working under challenging and difficult conditions. Her personal life included three marriages, a daughter, and a vast and varied group of friends. Julie Castiglia's liberal uses of quotes, numerous photographs, and inviting writing style capture this spirited, determined woman who lived her own life, despite the conventions of her time.

Marie Curie and Her Daughter Irène, Rosalynd Pflaum, 1993, *France*, BIOGRAPHY, *135 pages*

Seamlessly weaving together the personal and professional lives of Marie Curie and her daughter Irène Joliot-Curie, Rosalynd Pflaum offers an insightful dual biography. The dedication that the shy and impoverished Marie shows while pursuing her goal of a scientific education is only one of her strengths. In 1893, the first woman to receive a physics degree from the Sorbonne, she graduated at the top of her class; in 1894, she received a degree in mathematics. After their marriage, Marie and Pierre Curie conducted research on radioactivity in laboratories that were considered inadequate even then. In 1903, their work was acknowledged with the Nobel Prize in physics. In 1911, the first scientist to be honored twice, Marie Curie won a Nobel Prize in chemistry. Irène was born in 1897. By nature a serious person, she worked closely with her mother; they often closed their letters with equations to be solved. Irène became a scientist in her own right and in 1935, she and her husband, Frederic Joliot-Curie, were also awarded the Nobel Prize. Both women used their power to help others: Marie to aid her native Poland, and Irène to further women's causes in France. This well-written biography, both educational and entertaining, is above all inspirational.

Marked by Fire, Joyce Carol Thomas, 1982, *United States*, FICTION, *172 pages*

A grand and mystical feeling pervades *Marked by Fire.* The story tells of tornadoes, insanity, and the deep love between parents and child, husband and wife, women and their friends. Abyssinia is born in the cotton fields in 1951, one day after a tornado plows a circle around her mother and the other field hands, leaving them untouched. Abby grows up the beloved child of most of the town; when she sings in church, people cry at the beauty of her voice. Like the tornado that destroys her father's barbershop and his sanity, her rape by a neighbor is horrifying and unpredictable. Through the vast, powerful love and understanding of her mother and godmother, Abyssinia survives and learns to heal others in this stunning novel.

> *"You are an arrow in the bow of a benevolent wind."*
> *"What?" asked Abby, now listening intently.*
> *"My child, there is no greater joy on earth than the joy of healing."*
>
> from Marked by Fire *by Joyce Carol Thomas*

Mary Lincoln's Dressmaker: Elizabeth Keckley's Remarkable Rise from Slave to White House Confidante, Becky Rutberg, *1995, United States,* BIOGRAPHY, *158 pages*

Elizabeth Keckley spent thirty-seven years of her life as a slave. Passed around among her master's family, she was ordered about, whipped, and forced to have a child with a white man. Her skills as a dressmaker were used to make money for her owners. Finally she was allowed to buy her and her son's freedom for $1,200, a sum loaned to her by her loyal dressmaking patrons. Once free, she rose rapidly in society through her skills as a seamstress, and ultimately became Mary Lincoln's dressmaker and friend. Becky Rutberg's biography, accompanied by photographs, follows Elizabeth Keckley's remarkable life, and in doing so tells much about the Civil War era, Abraham Lincoln, and his nervous and sometimes irrational wife. Older readers may wish to look at Elizabeth Keckley's own eloquent 1868 account, *Behind the Scenes.*

A Matter of Conscience: The Trial of Anne Hutchinson, Joan Kane Nichols, illustrated by Dan Krovatin, *1993, United States,* BIOGRAPHY, *93 pages*

In 1634, Anne Hutchinson and her family left England to follow minister John Cotton to the Puritan colonies in the New World. For Anne Hutchinson, no other minister preached so clearly the doctrine she believed in—that people were saved from hell not because of external actions but because they were chosen by God and had an inward communion with Christ. Once in the Boston colony, she established meetings for women, in which she explained the sermons from the previous Sunday. These meetings grew from six to more than sixty people, and she had to add another group to accommodate men. After ignoring a synod rule against public meetings, she was put on trial and banished, despite her own eloquent defense. Joan Nichols draws from trial transcripts and histories to create a portrait of a strong and intelligent woman who took a stand against the power structure of her time.

The Midwife's Apprentice, Karen Cushman, *1995, Europe,* FICTION, *122 pages*

In *The Midwife's Apprentice,* Karen Cushman takes contemporary issues of identity and self-confidence and places them within an atmosphere rich in the sights, smells, sounds, and attitudes of the Middle Ages. As the book begins, a homeless orphan girl named Beetle, discovered sleeping in a dung heap, is taken home by a sharp-nosed, greedy midwife who sees her as an exploitable source of labor. Over time, as Beetle is sent on errands or eavesdrops on birthings, she learns the midwife's trade. But before Beetle can become a midwife, and before she can become a loving and giving human being, she must learn to believe in herself and her aspirations, a process full of intriguing plot twists and small steps. As Beetle renames herself Alyce, delivers twin calves, learns to read, takes her first real bath, helps an orphan, and stands up to the town bullies and later to the midwife, her story glows with affirmation while remaining steadfastly realistic in its portrayal of the difficulties of everyday life in the Middle Ages.

Miracles on Maple Hill, Virginia Sorensen, *1956, United States,* FICTION, *180 pages*

Ten-year-old Marly hopes that Maple Hill, her grandparents' old and now vacant farm in Pennsylvania, will make everything all right.

At Maple Hill, where there is "all outdoors," "there couldn't be very much indoors where all the trouble is." Maybe Father will be himself again, the way he was before he went to fight overseas in the war. Maybe she and her brother will get along and Mother will be happy. For Marly, Maple Hill has to be magic. And it is. There's Mr. Chris, their elderly neighbor, who knows the names and needs of every plant; there's the creaky farmhouse that makes Marly's father hurry around with a hammer in his hand and plans in his head. Most of all, there's all outdoors, to heal wounds and awaken everyone's curiosity.

> *Just the knowledge that a good book is awaiting one at the end of a long day makes that day happier.*
>
> *Kathleen Norris, writer*

Missing May, Cynthia Rylant, *1992, United States,* FICTION, *89 pages*

In her 1993 Newbery Award winner, *Missing May*, Cynthia Rylant addresses the issues of love, death, and renewal with a sure and steady hand. *Missing May* is narrated by twelve-year-old Summer, six months after her Aunt May has died. Six years before, May, who was "a big barrel of nothing but love," and her husband, Ob, brought Summer to their West Virginia home. It didn't matter that May and Ob were old enough to be Summer's grandparents, everything had been great—poor as they were, living in a dilapidated trailer with an old car rusting in the front yard. For Summer, who was a baby when her mom died, and was then passed around by her Ohio relations, May and Ob provided her first real home. But now Summer watches Ob slowly lose his will to live—it's too hard without May—and she feels yet another loss in her young life. With the help of an odd boy from school who reaches out to Ob in a way Summer is unable to, Ob and Summer find reasons to live and learn the importance of remembering May.

The Moon and I, Betsy Byars, *1991, United States,* MEMOIR, *94 pages*

Bull snakes, a goat named Butsy, museum mummies, miniature Snickers, The First Skateboard in the History of the World—put them all together and you get one author's personal and often humorous view of her writing process. Betsy Byars, the author of more than forty books, shares with readers the secrets of how she writes. She shows you her drawer filled with title pages and ideas; explains why so many of her mean characters are named Bubba; talks about plot, characters, and rejection—all in a down-to-earth voice that is filled with joy in her profession. Framing her discussion with a series of encounters with a large bull snake, she draws the reader into her own curiosity and eccentricities. Useful and entertaining, *The Moon and I* is a marvelous find for aspiring young writers and for teachers who are looking for a book to inspire creativity.

> *The organized soul has one book beside the bed. The glutton sleeps with a New York skyline lurching an inch from the bed.*
>
> Charlotte Gray, poet

The Moved-Outers, Florence Crannell Means, *1945, United States,* FICTION, *156 pages*

On December 7, 1941, the Japanese bombed Pearl Harbor. Eighteen-year-old Sumiko Ohara—"Sue"—an American citizen of Japanese ancestry, and her family are forced to leave their home for relocation centers set up by the government. In the internment camp, located in a desert and surrounded by barbed-wire fences, entire families live in rooms 16 by 24 feet, with water and bathrooms a block away. Sue, an eternal optimist, works hard to make the best of a bad situation. Kim, her younger brother, cannot hide his anger at the unjust treatment of Japanese-American people. First published in 1945, the year the war and the internment camps ended, *The Moved-Outers* is a good introduction to the internment of Japanese-

Americans as it explores both the myriad sacrifices of the internees and the enduring human need to make a home.

Mustang, Wild Spirit of the West, Marguerite Henry, *1966, United States,* BIOGRAPHICAL FICTION, *218 pages*

Marguerite Henry has written some of the best horse books around. *Mustang* is based on the true story of "Wild Horse Annie"— Annie Johnston—who started a crusade in the late 1950s to save the wild mustangs of Nevada. Annie grew up around horses and they created a firm foundation in her life that helped her withstand a cruel bout with polio. When she learned that the mustangs near her ranch were being rounded up by airplanes, killed, and ground into pet food, she reacted first with rage, and then with an increasingly well-orchestrated national campaign. This is a portrait of an ordinary woman made heroic by circumstance and by her connection with these beautiful wild animals.

The Nancy Drew Files: The Perfect Plot, Carolyn Keene, *1992, United States,* FICTION, *150 pages*

Since the first Nancy Drew mystery was published in 1930, Carolyn Keene's series featuring the quick-thinking and intrepid teenage detective has become an institution. Because Carolyn Keene is a pseudonym for a group of writers and because different collections have been created for more or less sophisticated audiences, the writing varies from book to book. *The Perfect Plot,* for example, has a complicated story line, multiple suspects, a house full of secret passages that come into play throughout the book, and a generally fluid writing style. In almost every Nancy Drew mystery, however, those who love a graceful sentence may find themselves wincing at regular intervals. But sixty-five years of fans care not at all for such criticism. For many readers, now adults, Nancy was an intelligent, adventurous role model back when there were few to choose from. For readers today, she remains a dynamic and resourceful young woman, able to pick a lock or outsmart the meanest villain.

National Velvet, Enid Bagnold, illustrated by Paul Brown, *1935, England,* FICTION, *306 pages*

National Velvet is a champion among horse books. It centers on fourteen-year-old Velvet, the "plain one" of four sisters, who has a rare understanding of horses. When Velvet wins for a shilling a piebald horse that jumps fences for fun, she starts on a journey toward the Grand National, a premier horse race in England. *National Velvet* portrays Velvet's quirky and fiercely loyal family, Velvet's unflinching belief in her horse, and the uproar she causes when she dresses as a boy to enter, and then wins, the Grand National. Following the conversations and keeping track of the numerous family characters can make for difficult reading in the beginning, but stick with it; once the book gathers its stride and focuses on Velvet and her ambition, it's a thrilling and inspiring story.

No Big Deal, Ellen Jaffe McClain, *1994, United States,* FICTION, *185 pages*

Despite comments from others, Janice strives to be her own person. She knows that reacting to Kevin Lynch's taunts of "Baby Huey" will only feed his fire, and that even if everyone is bored in math class, at times it's easier just to give the answer. Clothes shopping with her mom is a disaster; Janice wants big and loose, her mom suggests fitted and stylish, reassuring Janice that her baby fat will eventually disappear. When Janice hears rumors that her favorite teacher, Mr. Padovano (Mr. P), is gay, Janice thinks it's no big deal. But this rumor takes on a life of its own—Mr. P's car is vandalized, he becomes distant in his teaching style, parents meet to discuss his removal from school, and even Janice's mother wonders aloud if he should continue teaching. Ellen McClain's honest writing, sprinkled with humor and insight, develops her characters so that we understand many of their fears and reactions, while we grow with Janice, who at thirteen learns to trust both her head and her heart.

One More River, Lynne Reid Banks, *1973, Israel,* FICTION, *243 pages*

At fourteen, Lesley is pretty satisfied with her life; she does well at school and sports, her family is financially comfortable, and she has a new boyfriend. When her parents say they are moving to Israel, her spoiled nature rises to the surface. She knows she is Jewish—her family goes to synagogue and keeps kosher—but to leave Canada and move to Israel? *One More River* is the engrossing story of Lesley and Israel during the year 1967. In Israel, Lesley's family lives on a kibbutz, where parents sleep away from their children and everyone has a job. While Lesley struggles with the changes in her life that at times frighten her and listens to rumors of impending war, she comes to appreciate a fullness of life seen through differences and to understand that she can contribute to society. Inspirational and thought-provoking, *One More River* gives insights into both one girl's life and one country's history.

The Other Side of Silence, Margaret Mahy, *1995, New Zealand,* FICTION, *170 pages*

Hero, the narrator of *The Other Side of Silence,* writes that she quit speaking about three years ago when she was nine. It seemed the best way to deal with her unconventional, intelligent, and at times overpowering family. Though she's had numerous tests at school, they say that the longer it goes on, the less likely she is ever to speak again. But Hero is not particularly worried about it; she can and occasionally does speak to her brother. To her there are two worlds; the real and the true. The real is day-to-day life, while the true is what's going on in her mind. Then two things happen that change Hero's controlled existence. Her sister returns home after being away for three years, bringing an abandoned child and her own secrets, and Hero takes a gardening job working for an eccentric neighbor who has her own real and true worlds. It's when Hero's world collides with her neighbor's that Hero finds a use for her voice. *The Other Side of Silence* is a suspenseful and scary novel that draws the reader into the mysteries surrounding Hero.

Our Golda: The Story of Golda Meir, David A. Adler, illustrated by Donna Ruff, *1984, Israel,* BIOGRAPHY, *52 pages*

Golda Meir was born in 1898, into a hard life and a strong-willed Russian family. In her home there was always talk about the need for a Jewish homeland; too often Jewish people were attacked by soldiers and workers while the police looked on. In 1906, her family moved to the United States. Golda was a bright, determined girl, who at fourteen ran away to Denver to continue her schooling rather than follow her parents' wishes and marry an older man. In 1921, she and her husband of choice moved to Palestine, living for a time on a kibbutz and eventually settling in Jerusalem. There Golda continued her long and heartfelt work for a Jewish homeland, and for peace once Israel was established. A natural-born speaker, Golda's speeches won the respect and admiration of both world leaders and ordinary citizens. In 1969, she became the prime minister of Israel, a position she held for five years. *Our Golda* informs and entertains without shying away from the difficulties encountered with the birthing of a nation, a process greatly aided by this remarkable, resolute woman.

> *"Just remember that sometimes, when we patch our broken dreams together, they look a little different than they did before they were broken. But, they still hold fast."*
> from Out of Many Waters *by Jacqueline Dembar Greene*

Out of Many Waters, Jacqueline Dembar Greene, *1988, Brazil and United States,* HISTORICAL FICTION, *196 pages*

In 1648, a five-year-old Jewish girl named Isobel is kidnapped from her Portuguese home by the Inquisition and taken to Brazil; six years later, she escapes the Catholic friars and stows away aboard *The Valck.* By this time Isobel remembers little of her Jewish heritage; all she wants is to find her family again. But after she is discovered on board, it is Jewish refugees also fleeing the Inquisition in Brazil who take her in and care for her. When *The Valck* is captured by Spanish privateers who plan to turn the Jews over to the Inquisition, Isobel must make a difficult decision. Will she hide her identity and try to save herself, or will she stand with those who have given her a new sense of her own traditions? Isobel's desperate flight is full of suspense, and her growth into a strong and mature young woman is effectively chronicled. And while Isobel's character is fictional, the story comes out of the real-life history of twenty-three Jewish refugees who eventually evaded their Spanish captors and settled in New Amsterdam in 1654.

Out of the Blue, Sarah Ellis, *1995, United States,* FICTION, *120 pages*

Megan can tell something is going on, especially with her mother. Sneaking around her mom's file cabinet, she comes across a flyer about a boating excursion and thinks it is her gift for her twelfth birthday. Instead, over the weekend of her birthday, she finds out that her mom gave a daughter up for adoption twenty-four years ago and now this daughter has contacted her. Megan is furious about her mom's long-held secret. In the course of this honestly and beautifully written novel, Megan sorts through her complicated feelings. She knows she needs "some room to take out her tangled thoughts and have a look at them." She feels betrayed by her parents, as if they have lied, "maybe not in words but in silence." Her mother senses Megan's apprehensions and tries to help her, but she's confused, too, and Megan has wrapped herself up in her anger. It's a time of great upheaval for Megan and her mother, and when they come out the other end, they are both stronger and more defined people.

Owl in Love, Patrice Kindl, *1993, United States,* FANTASY, *204 pages*

Owl is teenager by day and owl by night, a shapeshifter, a were-owl in love with her science teacher. In the daytime, she observes him in class; at night, she sits in the tree outside his window and watches him sleep before reluctantly flying off to hunt for a meal of mice or other animals. Her divided existence puts Owl on the outside of everyday teenage activities. On this level, the book operates as a humorous exposé of human behavior, as Owl observes adolescence from the perspective of an owl. But there is a more serious side to the book. Owl is not the only one watching her teacher. A boy has come, ragged and troubled, and is hiding in the woods near her teacher's house. Owl can't decide who needs protecting, her teacher or the boy. The twin questions of the identity of the boy and of whether Owl—with her gray skin, unusual social skills, and abnormal eating habits—can pass as a human teenager unravel with well-timed suspense, and make for an entertaining and provocative book.

Patience and Sarah, Isabel Miller, *1969, United States,* FICTION, *215 pages*

Patience and Sarah was inspired by the lives of Mary Ann Wilson, an American primitive painter who lived in Greene County, New York, in the early nineteenth century, and her companion Miss Brundidge. When the novel begins, Patience is twenty-seven and still unmarried, living with her brother and his wife. One day she meets Sarah, who arrives dressed in men's clothes to deliver wood. The two fall deeply in love and plan to move away and buy their own farm. That decision would have been difficult for any two women in the early nineteenth century to carry out, but when the two women are lesbians and the families find out, all hell breaks loose. Eventually, after overcoming many internal and external obstacles, Patience and Sarah achieve their dream. Told from their alternating perspectives, the novel brings us a full understanding of their committed, sensual, and constantly evolving relationship.

The Perilous Gard, Elizabeth Marie Pope, illustrated by Richard Cuffari, *1974, England,* FANTASY, *280 pages*

The Perilous Gard is a real treat for those who love intricate story lines, blunt and resourceful heroines, and a rich historical setting. It starts with beautiful, dim-witted Alicia and her awkward and intelligent sister Kate, in service to Princess Elizabeth, who has been effectively made a prisoner by her sister Queen Mary. When Kate herself is banished to a remote castle, she is thrown into a world of dangerous fairy people, a lost child, a brooding man named Christopher, a magic well, suspicious villagers, and an obviously untrustworthy steward of the house. Drawn to Christopher, Kate tries to unravel the mystery surrounding him, only to be caught in it herself. Taken into the dark and terrifying underground by the fairy people, and relying only on her own courage and remarkable common sense, Kate must save herself and Christopher. Her levelheaded character and an admirably complex plot make for a substantial and satisfying novel.

> *What do books bring to my life? Connection, inspiration, solace, escape, entertainment, knowledge, joy, new worlds.*
> *Barbara Abercrombie, writer*

Picking Up the Pieces, Patricia Calvert, *1993, United States,* FICTION, *166 pages*

Since the motorcycle accident eight months ago, Megan's life has changed completely. A spinal cord injury has paralyzed her from the waist down and she is angry at the world and herself and burdened with feeling responsible for the stress and strain her family has endured. These days a shower that used to take ten minutes now takes forty-five; there are ramps at the house for her wheelchair, but she doesn't want to go outside. When her parents want to revisit a summer cottage, all Megan can think about is the hassle she will be. Patricia Calvert has given us a character who is frustrated and selfish, going through adolescent angst; she takes two steps forward, one step back, or in Megan's case, two spins forward, one spin back. Thank goodness for a little brother, the boy next door, and an older woman who can't face up to her own aging. Each in their own way helps Megan to see all that she can accomplish by herself, and to learn that offers of help aren't offers of pity.

Prairie Songs, Pam Conrad, illustrated by Daryl S. Zudeck, *1985, United States,* FICTION, *167 pages*

For many, pioneer life was a chance to live out a myth of adventure. But for others, many of them women, pioneer life meant the heartbreak of leaving family, friends, and comfortable homes. *Prairie Songs* is about two families on the Midwestern prairie. The only life young Louisa has known is one of sod houses, harsh winters, and Indian scares. When the new doctor and his wife, Emmeline, arrive from New York City, Louisa is awestruck by Emmeline's beauty and sophistication. Yet it soon becomes obvious that Emmeline will never be able to endure a life of cow chips, loneliness, and leaky roofs. As Louisa watches Emmeline slowly lose her sanity, she gains insight into another side of her own competent, resilient mother.

> *When I was nine years old, I hid under a table and heard my sister kill a king.*
>
> *from* Quest for a Maid *by Frances Mary Hendry*

Quest for a Maid, Frances Mary Hendry, *1988, Scotland,* HISTORICAL FICTION, *270 pages*

Quest for a Maid takes place in thirteenth-century Scotland, during the reign of King Alexander III and the tumultuous years that followed his death. Margaret Wright's sister has powers, and she uses them to cause the king's death and advance her own position. Margaret is strong, brave, and sure to speak up when she shouldn't. When she saves the life of a rich man's son, she is promised to him in marriage. All goes fairly well until Margaret is sent to Norway to bring back the young princess, granddaughter of King Alexander. This is a book to carry off to your favorite reading place, for there are storms and shipwrecks, intrigue and chases, sisterly love and revenge, and plenty of period details.

The Rain Catchers, Jean Thesman, *1991, United States,* FICTION, *182 pages*

It is the summer of Grayling's fourteenth year, a summer she will learn about first love, death, family, and friendship. Grayling lives in a houseful of women headed by her grandmother, and it is at teatime that they tell stories. These compassionate, practical women like a good laugh, and as they reminisce about and reexamine embarrassments, divorces, lost loves, and family histories, they derive comfort from the retelling. Grayling knows that stories have a beginning, a middle, and an end, yet she feels her own story is incomplete. What happened to her mother that night shortly after Grayling's father was killed? Why doesn't Grayling live with her? Not that Grayling minds her home; she is surrounded by hearty, caring women whom she loves and who love her. Jean Thesman, author of several books with strong female characters, weaves another realistic tale as Grayling learns about her own story and discovers that she can be a storyteller too.

> *It should be possible to exist with only a short shelf of books, to read and give away. After all—we may not open a book, once read, for ten years or more. But the act of reading has made it part of us—to relinquish it would be to lose an extension of being.*
>
> Pamela Brown, writer

The Ramsay Scallop, Frances Temple, *1994, England and France,* HISTORICAL FICTION, *310 pages*

It is 1299 and fourteen-year-old Elenor waits with foreboding for the return of her husband-to-be who left to fight in the Crusades eight years before. When Thomas arrives, he is heartsick over his role in the wars and no more enthusiastic about the wedding than she. The wise Father Gregory sends the pair on a pilgrimage from England to Santiago do Compostela in Spain, ostensibly to atone for the sins of the villagers. On the way, they meet many and varied people, and as their minds widen, so do the possibilities for their future. The pilgrimage and their growing love for each other provide the foundation for a novel that is filled with interesting facts, stories, and beliefs from seven hundred years ago.

The Reason for Janey, Nancy Hope Wilson, *1994, United States,* FICTION, *160 pages*

Philly likes to know the reason for things. Last year when she won first place at her fifth-grade science fair, she thought the blue ribbon was nice, but more than that, she liked knowing the reason for rain, the basis of her experiment. Eight months ago, Janey moved into her house, and Philly can't help but wonder why Janey, who is a mentally handicapped adult, fits in better than Philly's dad, who moved out three years ago. The novel unfolds through Philly's school days, home life, and weekend trips to her dad's. Philly learns that Janey has a father who doesn't want her. When Philly's plan to reunite Janey with her father backfires, Philly slowly, painfully, recognizes her anger at her own father and grapples with the difficult issues of abandonment and acceptance. Philly comes to understand that the hopes she has for others aren't necessarily their hopes, that parents aren't perfect and have pasts of their own, and eventually, that dreams become steps on a growing-up path.

The Return, Sonia Levitin, *1987, Ethiopia and Israel,* HISTORICAL FICTION, *178 pages*

Between November 1984 and January 1985, a dangerous secret airlift between Sudan and Israel rescued eight thousand black Jews from persecution in Ethiopia. *The Return* is a fictionalized account of one family's escape. Desta is sixteen when she, her brother, and her sister leave their village in the mountains and begin their perilous, at times terrifying, escape to Sudan. The brother is killed, and when Desta and her sister finally reach Sudan, they are put into camps with other refugees who hope to find a way to Israel. What this novel explains so profoundly is how religion defines life for Desta and her family. Persecution by the Ethiopian government and non-Jewish citizens has made Desta realize she must go. To leave one's family, village, country, never to return, and to do that at sixteen, takes amazing courage. *The Return* is a compelling, complex novel, highly recommended for older readers.

> *The novel is a rescued life.*
>
> Hortense Calisher, *writer*

Rice Without Rain, Minfong Ho, *1990, Thailand,* HISTORICAL FICTION, *236 pages*

In the village of Maekung, a farmer's rent has always been one-half of the rice harvest. This year there has been little rain and seventeen-year-old Jinda knows that after her family pays rent, they won't have enough rice to last until the next harvest. When four university students arrive in her village, they bring with them the revolutionary idea of paying the landlords only one-third of the harvest. It's an idea that divides the village, and when Jinda's father gives the landlord one-third, he is imprisoned. *Rice Without Rain* is a full-bodied novel that explores Jinda's responsibilities to her family and the ideas that outsiders bring. The students are the first nonvillagers Jinda has met: Sri brings new medicines, and her warm spirit attracts Jinda; Ned has enthusiasm and democratic ideas that Jinda admires. Based on actual events in Thai history, *Rice Without Rain* shows class struggles through Jinda's perspective as she has to decide what is worth fighting for.

The Road from Home: The Story of an Armenian Girl, David Kherdian, *1979, Turkey,* BIOGRAPHICAL FICTION, *238 pages*

"For as long as I knew the sky and the clouds, we lived in our white stucco house in the Armenian quarter of Azizya, in Turkey, but when the great dome of Heaven cracked and shattered over our lives, and we were abandoned by the sun and blown like scattered seed across the Arabian desert, none returned but me." In 1915, when David Kherdian's mother, Veron, was eight years old, her community was torn apart as Armenians were rounded up and taken from their homes. Many died during forced marches; many others, including most of Veron's family, died of disease. Veron was lucky, and eventually she made it to the United States. Speaking eloquently in his mother's voice, David Kherdian relates a little-known portion of world history in this beautiful and troubling book.

The Roller Birds of Rampur, Indi Rana, *1993, India,* FICTION, *309 pages*

At the age of seven, Sheila and her family moved from their multigenerational home in Rampur, India, to London, England. Ten years have passed, and while Sheila has been back for visits with her parents, she is now in Rampur without them, thinking hard about her future. A many-layered novel, *The Roller Birds of Rampur* explores through Sheila's eyes issues of life, destiny, and choice. Sheila, feeling completely out of balance with herself and thinking she is coming home, finds herself a stranger in India, with its caste system and obvious poverty, a place where riches are not necessarily measured with material goods and modernization has had its own profound impact. Talks with her grandfather revolve around karma, dharma, acceptance, and responsibility. Sheila is a curious, confused, and smart young woman, confronting life's philosophical challenges for the first time.

> *People always say that I didn't give up my seat because I was tired, but that wasn't true . . . the only tired I was, was tired of giving in.*
>
> *from* Rosa Parks: My Story *by Rosa Parks*

Rosa Parks: My Story, Rosa Parks with Jim Haskins, *1992, United States,* AUTOBIOGRAPHY, *188 pages*

Most people associate Rosa Parks with one incident in the Civil Rights movement of the 1950s and '60s—when she refused to relinquish her seat on a segregated Montgomery, Alabama, bus. In fact, Rosa Parks resisted racism and was active in civil rights protests throughout her life, from her childhood refusal to be bullied by white children, through her determination to register to vote (it took three attempts), her membership as one of two women in her chapter of the NAACP, her active participation in the year-long bus boycott that followed her arrest in 1955, and her speeches and teaching. Rosa Parks is an articulate, inspiring woman and her autobiography provides a first-person view of the Civil Rights movement in the twentieth century.

The Ruby in the Smoke, Philip Pullman, *1985, England,* FICTION, *230 pages*

It is a cold afternoon in October 1872. A sixteen-year-old girl gets out of a hansom cab and pays the driver: "Her name was Sally Lockart; and within fifteen minutes, she was going to kill a man." And for 230 pages the mystery plunges along, propelled by an evil opium trader, a wicked old woman named Mrs. Holland, a lost ruby, plots of revenge, a handsome photographer, and Sally, an intrepid orphan with a knack for mathematics. A mysterious note from her father, now dead, sends Sally on a search which soon places her in harm's way. Those who were meant to help her all fail, and assistance instead comes from unlikely sources—a Cockney errand boy, whose reading of "penny dreadfuls" helps solve more than one puzzle, and Frederick Garland, whose photography business needs her accounting skills as much as she needs the shelter and friendship he offers. It is all fast-paced and terribly exciting, and, luckily for readers, there's a sequel.

A Rumour of Otters, Deborah Savage, *1984, New Zealand,* FICTION, *156 pages*

Fourteen-year-old Alexa knows she is capable of helping with the sheep roundup on her family's remote New Zealand farm. She is more familiar with the land and is a better rider than her brother, but because he is two years older and a boy, he gets to go. Alexa doesn't want to stay with her mom, stuck with the baby and the day-to-day chores of the station. Frustrated by her situation, and obsessed with a legend of otters living in a remote mountain lake, Alexa sets off with an old horse and little food to find out the truth for herself. Through sheer determination, she confronts both physical and emotional obstacles and finds the otters that few others believe actually exist. But it's the lessons she learns while on her quest—about her family, nature, animals, and, of course, herself—that readers will find compelling.

Runaway to Freedom, Barbara Smucker, illustrated by Charles Lilly, *1977, United States,* HISTORICAL FICTION, *152 pages*

Twelve-year-old Julilly has spent her childhood as a slave on Massa Henson's farm. Life is hard but not brutal until Julilly is sold south, away from her mother. On Master Riley's plantation, slaves are routinely whipped, small children eat at a trough, and Julilly sleeps on a pile of rags with the other slave girls in a long, dark shack. There she befriends Liza, hunchbacked and weakened from beatings, and the two of them make a pact to escape to Canada. Their flight is made possible through their own refusal to give up, a good disguise, and the assistance of the Underground Railroad. Informative about both the Underground Railroad and the issues of slavery, *Runaway to Freedom* is also a well-told narrative with powerful characters.

> *A book is like a garden carried in the pocket.*
>
> *Chinese proverb*

The Secret Garden, Frances Hodgson Burnett, *1911, England,* FICTION, *256 pages*

Few books so beautifully capture and celebrate the transformative power of spring and nature as *The Secret Garden.* The story follows Mary Lennox, a spoiled and crabby child, as she moves from India to England to live an almost solitary existence at her uncle's manor, Misselthwaithe. Here, Mary's elitism and bad humor are disrupted by the good-natured common sense of a Yorkshire housemaid and her brother Dickon, who can communicate with animals. In a far corner of the mansion, Mary finds an unknown cousin who has been hidden away. Outside, she finds a secret garden. The change that the garden brings to Mary and her cousin is magical. Although many abridged editions are available, only the original version enables you to enjoy fully Frances Hodgson Burnett's glorious descriptions and lyrical prose.

Seven Daughters and Seven Sons, Barbara Cohen and Bahia Lovejoy, *1982, Iraq,* FICTION, *220 pages*

Based on an Iraqi folktale from the eleventh century, *Seven Daughters and Seven Sons* tells the story of Buran, fourth daughter of a poor shopkeeper stuck with seven daughters and no sons to help him with his business. After Buran's uncle scorns to marry any of his seven sons to their impoverished cousins, Buran manages to persuade her father to let her travel as a boy and become a merchant. The journey is hard; the training, more arduous still. Yet eventually Buran becomes a successful merchant, achieves revenge upon her seven male cousins, and gains the love of a prince. This is a great read—atmospheric, suspenseful, and driven by a brave and resourceful character.

> *My main disappointment was always that a book had to end.*
> *Eudora Welty, writer*

Shabanu: Daughter of the Wind, Suzanne Fisher Staples, *1989, Pakistan,* FICTION, *240 pages*

Shabanu lives in the Cholistan Desert of Pakistan with her parents, grandfather, and older sister Phulan. Thirteen-year-old Phulan's marriage is fast approaching; Shabanu's will follow soon after. Shabanu knows, even likes, her future groom, but she does not wish to give up her independence or her work helping her father care for their herd of camels. While Phulan prepares for marriage, becoming a person Shabanu hardly recognizes, Shabanu cherishes her hours away from the house, out in the wilderness of the desert or accompanying her father on a trading journey. Still, there is no way she can avoid what is coming. Shabanu's inner struggles are universal, made fresh by the richly detailed setting and a mesmerizing story.

Shizuko's Daughter, Kyoko Mori, *1993, Japan,* FICTION, *218 pages*

Perhaps if twelve-year-old Yuki had come home early from her piano lesson, she could have stopped her mother's suicide. Yuki remembers her mother as a warm and happy woman; now she realizes her mother had another side. After her father remarries, Yuki finds herself living with a silent father and a stepmother who doesn't understand her quiet, powerful stepdaughter, and soon resents her. Yuki is determined to learn from her past. She spends time remembering her parents' marriage and her mother; she thinks about the conversations they had together and learns self-reliance and hope from the heart. Forced to grow up quickly, she has difficulties, but she also has focus—on her art, her mother's family, and her work to understand her mother's life. Kyoko Mori's insightful, poetic writing brings alive Yuki's adolescence and the blossoming of her maturity.

So Young to Die: The Story of Hannah Senesh, Candice F. Ransom, *1993, Hungary and Israel,* BIOGRAPHY, *145 pages*

Born in Hungary in 1921, Hannah Senesh was a happy, bright, conscientious young girl. As Hitler rose to power in Europe, her Jewish heritage became the defining factor of her life; she studied Hebrew and at age eighteen followed her dream and went to Palestine to help settle a Jewish homeland. There she worked hard at agricultural school and on the kibbutz. But the effects of the war in Europe were also felt in Palestine, and Hannah could not forget that her mother, who was still in Hungary, was now behind enemy lines. In 1943, Hannah joined the British Air Force and eventually was sent to Europe on a secret rescue mission to parachute behind enemy lines. She landed in Yugoslavia, sneaked into Hungary, was captured, imprisoned, and eventually executed. *So Young to Die* is a compelling narrative, peppered with Hannah's own diary entries. In her brief life she proved herself to be a compassionate, courageous person who felt called to know and give more.

> *A great book reaches over the wall of experience and tells me something I didn't know.*
>
> Tom Gjelten, *reporter and writer*

Sojourner Truth and the Struggle for Freedom, Edward Beecher Claflin, illustrated by Jada Rowland, *1987, United States,* BIOGRAPHY, *142 pages*

During the first thirty years of her life, Sojourner Truth was sold away from her parents, whipped, married to a man she didn't love, and promised a freedom that was not delivered. When she finally gained her freedom, she used it powerfully. She went to court to challenge the man who sold her son, integrated the Washington, D.C., streetcars, and campaigned relentlessly after the Civil War for ex-slaves to be given land in the Midwest. Through it all, she proved she was a speaker. Six feet tall, with a voice that rolled out over a room, she mesmerized crowds as she spoke out passionately for equal rights for all human beings. Students of history and humanity alike will find much to inspire them in her biography.

Song of Be, Lesley Beake, *1993, Namibia,* FICTION, *94 pages*

For generation upon generation, the Bushmen of the Kalahari Desert lived with the land. Then the government drafted some of the men as wartime trackers, farmers came wanting land, traders brought things to buy, and government officials moved many people into settlements where jobs were few but alcohol was abundant. Be is coming to maturity as the country of Namibia is forming and must decide how its people will live. Be's story—her traditional life in the desert, her experiences on a white man's farm, her own emerging consciousness—is charged by the information given the reader at the beginning of the story that Be has poisoned herself and is waiting to die. While the context appears morbid, the book is stunning, highly educational, and ultimately hopeful.

A Sound of Chariots, Mollie Hunter, *1972, Scotland,* FICTION, *242 pages*

A Sound of Chariots is a wise book that deals articulately and insightfully with the loss of a beloved father and the effect it has on a sensitive, artistic young girl named Bridie as she grows into adulthood. Bridie's father is an Irishman, wounded in World War I, a socialist often in trouble for his politics. Bridie is his favorite child, and their relationship is lovingly portrayed. When he dies, Bridie must deal both with her own terrible grief and with the changes that occur to her gentle, devout mother and the rest of their family. Capturing the various stages of Bridie's mourning and growth, Mollie Hunter explores Bridie's evolution from a child who loves to play with words to a young woman who sees a purpose to writing and understands its beauty.

> *The greatest gift is the passion for reading.*
>
> *Elizabeth Hardwick, writer*

Sound the Jubilee, Sandra Forrester, *1995, United States,* HISTORICAL FICTION, *183 pages*

When eleven-year-old Maddie's mistress takes her and her family to Nags Head, North Carolina, fleeing the oncoming Yankee soldiers, Maddie's family gets an unexpected opportunity. Northern soldiers take over nearby Roanoke Island, and Maddie's family escapes to freedom, a short boat ride away. On Roanoke, the self-freed slaves are given land and assistance in establishing their own lives and community. Finally, Maddie's family can build their own house, and Maddie sets up a school where she can teach the children to read. Not all is happy, however. Maddie's father goes off to join the army, some of the Northern soldiers are jealous of the treatment the former slaves are given, and eventually it becomes obvious that the government will return the land to the original owners. Through it all, Maddie grows from a stubborn and sometimes wayward child into a mature and giving human being as readers learn about little-known events from American history.

Steal Away . . . to Freedom, Jennifer Armstrong, *1992, United States,* FICTION, *207 pages*

Steal Away . . . to Freedom is the story as Susannah and Bethlehem tell it in 1896, when Bethlehem is on her deathbed. Susannah and her thirteen-year-old granddaughter Mary have traveled to Toronto to visit Bethlehem and her caregiver, a young woman named Free. Free and Mary record the alternating voices, and the story that unfolds to intertwine with theirs is a powerful, honest testimony of a time and place still fresh in these women's minds. In 1855, when she was thirteen, Susannah's parents died and her minister uncle came to Vermont to take her back to Virginia with him. Upon her arrival she was given Bethlehem, a girl near her own age, to be her slave. Susannah didn't believe in slavery; Bethlehem never knew anything else. Within months they escaped together heading north; Susannah was going home, Bethlehem to freedom. The courage and lessons they learned along the way reinforce the theme that life is not the destination but the journey.

> *And for conversation, Maria considered, things were infinitely preferable. Animals, frequently. Trees and plants, from time to time. Sometimes what they said was consoling, and sometimes it was uncomfortable, but at least you were having a conversation. For a real heart-to-heart, you couldn't do much better than a clock. For a casual chat, almost anything would do.*
>
> from A Stitch in Time *by Penelope Lively*

A Stitch in Time, Penelope Lively, *1976, England,* FICTION, *149 pages*

Maria is a quiet and thoughtful only child given to having involved, two-way conversations with gas station pumps and cats. Her parents are, if possible, more taciturn than she, and their vacation in Lyme Regis is very quiet indeed until Maria discovers two things:

the sampler of a young girl who lived in their vacation house in 1865, and a rambunctious family staying at the hotel next door. Maria's relationship with nineteenth-century Harriet verges on the supernatural; her friendship with the noisy family is absolutely down-to-earth. Perhaps that's an odd combination, but it's just what Maria needs as she tries to figure out who she is, and it makes for a wonderfully eccentric book with an ending that is unexpectedly perfect.

The Store That Mama Built, Robert Lehrman, *1992, United States,* FICTION, *126 pages*

When twelve-year-old Birdie's father dies of influenza, he leaves behind a wife, six children, and a grocery store he was getting ready to open in a small Pennsylvania town. None of the children wants to return to New York City, where Mama's extended family lives, and together with Mama they decide to open the store on their own. For Mama, it means learning business practices, using English instead of Yiddish, and deciding if they will sell ham or close for Shabbas. For Birdie, the store becomes a lesson in overcoming discrimination and "common practice" as her family welcomes and then extends credit to the black people who live nearby. In the process, Birdie gains new respect for her mother and her strengths, comes to value her family's Jewish traditions, and learns to make decisions for herself, regardless of what her friends think.

Sweet Fifteen, Diana Gonzales Bertrand, *1995, United States,* FICTION, *296 pages*

Soon Stephanie will turn fifteen, and her mother and Uncle Brian are determined to give her a traditional Latina coming-of-age party, a *quinceañera,* following plans already begun when her loving but authoritarian father suddenly died six months ago. Stephanie feels as if her life is out of control; she doesn't want to be at Rita's dress shop. But as Rita sews, Stephanie talks and Rita becomes involved in Stephanie's and her family's lives. This is a novel about family, work, change, and the romantic love that develops between Rita and Brian. Over the two months covered in the book, each character learns some important things. Stephanie's mother gains an independence she's never had before. In opening his heart to others, Brian comes to understand the difference between supporting and controlling. Rita learns the strength of trusting herself. And Stephanie, caught in two cultures, begins to find a balance that brings her happiness.

The Talking Earth, Jean Craighead George, *1983, United States,* FICTION, *151 pages*

Jean Craighead George, author of *Julie of the Wolves* and *My Side of the Mountain,* is well-known for her interesting characters, exciting story lines, and detailed attention to the natural world. *The Talking Earth* concerns Billie Wind, a Seminole Indian sent out alone into the Everglades on a quest after she expresses doubt about legends of talking animals and earth spirits. A huge fire turns what was supposed to be an overnight trip into a several-week journey of discovery. Befriended by an otter, a panther cub, and a turtle, relying on every clue she can find for her survival, she learns to listen to the talking earth and its creatures.

> *"You are too practical," he said. "That is the white man's trait. There is more to the Earth than only things you can see with your eyes."*
>
> *"What are they?" she asked with great sincerity. "I would love to see what isn't there."*
>
> *from* The Talking Earth *by Jean Craighead George*

A Tree Grows in Brooklyn, Betty Smith, *1943, United States,* FICTION, *430 pages*

It's the summer of 1912, and the best part of eleven-year-old Francie Nolan's day is when she can escape with a book onto the fire escape of her Brooklyn, New York, tenement apartment home. Francie is a strong child, who faces the poverty of her surroundings, her father's alcoholism, and her mother's exhaustion from overwork and still finds much to love in the neighborhood around her. For Francie, the world is alive, no matter where you live. A big and satisfying novel, *A Tree Grows in Brooklyn* traces Francie's life as she grows into an intelligent, clear-eyed young woman.

Trouble's Child, Mildred Pitts Walter, *1985, United States,* FICTION, *157 pages*

Fourteen-year-old Martha lives on Blue Isle, off the coast of Louisiana, where tradition and superstition run as deep as the Gulf that surrounds their island. If you're born in a storm, like Martha was, you're born for trouble, and while most girls her age are putting out their quilting pattern, ready for marriage, Martha is disrupting tradition. All her life she has learned the midwife and healing arts from her grandmother, Titay; now Martha wants to leave the island and go to high school. Martha's dilemma and the courage of her decision will be recognizable to all, while the setting brings new insights into the issues of identity and independence.

The True Confessions of Charlotte Doyle, Avi, *1992, United States,* FICTION, *226 pages*

In this adventure book set in 1832, thirteen-year-old Charlotte Doyle finds herself the sole female passenger of the notorious ship *Seahawk*. While on board, she witnesses a murder, helps in a mutiny, becomes a sailor, and eventually is made captain. Although the events may seem implausible, readers relish Charlotte's metamorphosis from spoiled rich girl to one of the crew, the plot is exciting, and there is much to learn here about sailing and ships in the nineteenth century. The end provides a nice twist, as Charlotte-the-sailor encounters her affluent and well-mannered family upon her arrival in New England. Students who have encountered *Billy Budd* or *Moby-Dick* may appreciate this version of the conflict-at-sea story through Charlotte's eyes.

Truth to Tell, Nancy Bond, *1994, New Zealand,* FICTION, *325 pages*

Although Alice's mother explains that she wants to take this job offer, and that at forty-one she needs to make some changes, the last thing fourteen-year-old Alice wants to do is leave England and move to New Zealand. Upon their arrival they find nothing is as they expected. Instead of writing an architectural history of Florestan, the mansion they live in, her mother ends up as a housekeeper and caregiver to its owner, the elderly, reclusive Miss Fairchild. Alice's classmates are full of questions: Is Florestan really falling down? Is Miss Fairchild crazy? Then a comment by Miss Fairchild and a reaction from Alice's stepfather send Alice on a quest to seek the truth of something she has never questioned. On her journey she comes to understand that life is change and motion, and that truth is different from fact. With well-developed characters, interesting descriptions of the Dunedin area, and multiple story lines, *Truth to Tell* is a very satisfying read.

> *If I read a book that impresses me, I have to take myself firmly in hand before I mix with other people; otherwise they would think my mind rather queer.*
>
> Anne Frank, *writer*

Tuck Everlasting, Natalie Babbitt, *1975, United States,* FANTASY, *139 pages*

Winnie lives in a spotless cottage, her life controlled by her mother and grandmother. One day she runs away, but what she finds is not what she ever expected. In the woods behind her house there is a spring, and beside it a beautiful young man, Jesse Tuck. The spring has given him and his family immortality, and now she must stay with them until they are sure she won't share their secret. Winnie's brief time with the Tucks teaches her much about loyalty, friendship, and the necessity of death: "Dying's part of the wheel, right there next to being born. You can't pick out the pieces you like and leave the rest. Being part of the whole thing, that's the blessing." A strange and wonderful story, *Tuck Everlasting* reassures and provokes thought on many levels.

Walk Two Moons, Sharon Creech, *1994, United States,* FICTION, *280 pages*

It's been a difficult year for Salamanca Tree Hinkle—"Sal." She and her parents used to live on a farm with a barn, a swimming hole, and lots of trees. After the baby died, her mother left, and Sal and her father moved to a town three hundred miles away, leaving that home and her grandparents behind. Now Sal has met Phoebe Winterbottom, whose own strange life will help Sal unravel some of the confusions that being thirteen, missing your mother, and moving can bring. It's a friendship that is life-affirming in the midst of Sal's bewildering feelings. *Walk Two Moons* unfolds as Sal travels from Ohio to Idaho with her eccentric grandparents in search of her mother. Sal's curious and kind grandparents are a fine audience for her to tell Phoebe's story to and, in the process, remember her own.

The War Between the Classes, Gloria D. Miklowitz, *1985, United States,* FICTION, *158 pages*

The characters all fall into stereotypes: Amy Sumoto, the main character, is Asian-American, quiet and submissive, good in math. Her boyfriend Adam is an affluent, Greek-god look-alike; classmate Paul is black and frustrated; Juan has a loving family that makes nachos. But stereotypes are the point in this book, as these high school students take part in a sociology experiment that places them in different economic and social classes based on randomly chosen colored armbands. Amy finds herself a blue, the chosen class, while Adam becomes a lowly orange. In addition, because she is female, Amy is now in a privileged position. Trouble quickly arises and as the game progresses, each student learns a great deal about themselves, power, their capacity to hurt others, and their ability to resist authority.

Warriors Don't Cry: A Searing Memoir of the Battle to Integrate Little Rock's Central High, Melba Pattillo Beals, *1994, United States,* MEMOIR, *312 pages*

Almost forty years after she became one of nine students to integrate Little Rock's Central High, Melba Beals was finally able to write about her experience. Her memoir, which draws from the diary she kept and articles her mother clipped, makes it unequivocally clear that for these students, integration was war. Forced to endure continual verbal and physical assaults, "protected" by the Arkansas National Guard and school officials who preferred to ignore their torment, she still refused to quit school. Her account is effectively detailed and passionately written, a gripping and eye-opening read.

Where the Lilies Bloom, Vera and Bill Cleaver, illustrated by Jim Spunfeller, *1969, United States,* FICTION, *174 pages*

Mary Call is a fourteen-year-old girl with worries far beyond her age. Her mother is dead, her father is dying, and the family can barely pay the rent on their farm in the mountains of Appalachia. She knows in order to keep her family together she must make sure her father's death—when it finally happens—stays a secret. She also knows she must stall off the farmer who owns their land from marrying her cloudy-headed eighteen-year-old sister. And then there's her younger brother Romey and little Ima Dean to take care of. There's a lot to manage. But Mary Call is bright, stubborn, and determined. She will let no one break apart her family, and she is going to get an education. She draws on her own strength, and finds her solution in the mountains around her.

> *When I get trapped in a book, everything outside the pages disappears.*
>
> *Christine Lambert, middle school student*

White Lilacs, Carolyn Meyer, *1993, United States,* HISTORICAL FICTION, *237 pages*

In 1921, Rose Lee was living in Freedom, the part of Dillon, Texas, where the African-American people had their houses. Freedom is well-established, with schools, stores, churches, and Rose Lee's grandfather's garden, as beautiful as the original Eden. But Freedom is smack in the middle of Dillon, surrounded by the houses of white people who decide they want to eliminate the "eyesore" and replace it with a park. *White Lilacs,* based on the true story of Denton, Texas, follows Rose Lee through one long, hot summer, as she comes to understand what Freedom really means.

A Whole New Ball Game: The Story of the All-American Girls Professional Baseball League, Sue Macy, *1993, United States,* NON-FICTION, *128 pages*

Sue Macy begins with a historical overview of the professional women's baseball league that existed for twelve seasons between 1943 and 1954, then fills in the details and little-known facts that make this thoroughly researched story fascinating. Created during World War II when professional men's baseball was suffering from a loss of players to the military, the All-American Girls Professional Baseball League became a source of pride and entertainment for nearly a million people and a professional opportunity for many extremely talented athletes. The end of the war and subsequent changes in social attitudes which demanded that women return to the home meant the end of the AAGPBL, but as Sue Macy shows, the professional teams had a profound effect on the lives of these women and their audiences long after the League ended.

Wildflower Girl, Marita Conlon-McKenna, illustrated by Donald Teskey, *1991, Ireland and United States,* FICTION, *173 pages*

It is the 1850s, and Ireland is still suffering from the potato famine. Thirteen-year-old Peggy O'Driscoll comes to understand that emigrating to the United States may be her only hope for the future, even if she must travel alone and leave all her family behind. *Wildflower Girl* describes in realistic detail Peggy's grueling journey across the sea, her confusion when she lands in the new country, her disastrous first job as a servant for a drunken boardinghouse keeper, and her experience working in a fine house outside of the city. Peggy soon learns that the wealth of her employers does not guarantee her an easier position, but she has always been a resilient and determined girl—a self-described wildflower now trying to survive among society flowers—and it is clear she will eventually succeed.

Wise Child, Monica Furlong, *1987, Scotland,* FANTASY, *228 pages*

It is a long time ago. When Wise Child's grandmother dies, Wise Child is taken in by Juniper, the woman the villagers of this long-ago remote Scottish village see as a witch, albeit a good one. In Juniper's home, Wise Child learns about hard work, herbs, healing, and the value of seeing the interconnections among all life. There is evil in the form of Wise Child's mother, Maeve, who returns to the village and tries to lure Wise Child away. There is fear when smallpox turns the villagers against Juniper. In between there are broomstick rides, hidden caverns, and a lot of very down-to-earth lessons about living and generosity.

> *I hope heaven is a bookstore.*
>
> Missy Bird-Vogel, high school student

The Wolves of Willoughby Chase, Joan Aiken, illustrated by Pat Marriott, *1962, England,* FICTION, *168 pages*

A tongue-in-cheek version of nineteenth-century Gothic novels, *The Wolves of Willoughby Chase* is equally entertaining as satire or adventure. The novel begins in the dead of winter as high-spirited little Bonnie listens to the wolves howling outside her family's mansion and awaits the arrival of her sweet, impoverished cousin Sylvia. But Sylvia is not the only arrival. There is also the evil Miss Slighcarp, a distant relative who has come to take over while Bonnie's parents travel the world for Bonnie's mother's health. No sooner have the parents left than Miss Slighcarp begins dismissing loyal servants, burning legal wills, wearing Bonnie's mother's best dresses, and shutting Bonnie up in a cupboard. Despite all their efforts to be saved, Bonnie and Sylvia are packed off to a work-factory orphanage. But

Bonnie is intrepid, Sylvia is good, and evil will never be allowed to win in this fast-paced novel destined to please a wide range of ages.

A Woman Unafraid: The Achievements of Frances Perkins, Penny Colman, *1993, United States,* BIOGRAPHY, *110 pages*

Frances Perkins was the first woman to be appointed to a Cabinet post in the United States government—a position she held for twelve years, longer than any Cabinet minister but one in U.S. history. Penny Colman's biography focuses on Frances Perkins's college years, her post-college work for social reform at Hull House in Chicago, and her tenure as a member of the Industrial Commission of New York and later as the Secretary of Labor during Franklin Roosevelt's presidency. Opinionated and committed, a straight-talking woman who did not use her husband's name, she fought hard to better working conditions and ensure fair wages throughout the United States. Loaded with facts, this biography gives real insight into the creation of some of the most sweeping social reforms and legislation of the twentieth century—including Medicare and Social Security—while telling the story of a spirited, driven woman who achieved what many saw as impossible.

Women of the World: Women Travelers and Explorers, Rebecca Stefoff, *1992, Asia, Africa, Arctic, North America,* BIOGRAPHY, *143 pages*

Women of the World focuses on women from Europe and the United States who explored the world in the nineteenth and early twentieth centuries. Their life stories are almost as fascinating as the places they visited: Ida Pfeiffer took up traveling at the age of forty-five; Isabella Bird Bishop's health failed every time she stopped exploring. Alexandra David-Neel became, at age fifty-five, the first Western woman to see the Forbidden City in Tibet; Florence Baker, once a Hungarian slave, ended up searching for the source of the Nile; Louise Arner Boyd was an affluent socialite fascinated with the Arctic. Their ten- to fifteen-page biographies, liberally interspersed with photographs, engravings, and maps, are both informative and engaging. An afterword mentions more recent women explorers, while an extensive bibliography suggests further reading possibilities.

Fascinating and invigorating, this book makes a perfect gift for aspiring explorers.

> *Something always comes to fill the empty places. . . . Something comes to take the place of what you lose.*
> *from* Words by Heart *by Ouida Sebestyn*

Words by Heart, Ouida Sebestyen, *1979, United States,* FICTION, *135 pages*

Lena knows the Scriptures better than anybody, and she is determined to win the Bible-quoting contest to prove her talent: "Tonight was a special night, Lena's night, when her Magic Mind was going to matter, not her skin." But her small, turn-of-the-century Western town isn't ready for a black girl to win the contest, and some people, already resentful of Lena's father's work skills, use her victory as an opportunity to vent their racism. Lena's anger at the bigotry that surrounds her is tempered by her father's calm and dignity. Her frustration with white people is complicated by her emerging friendship with a white boy and by her new insights into her father's wealthy employer and the impoverished white family nearby. In a world without easy answers, in the midst of violence, goodness, and sacrifice, Lena must find her own way. A wise and powerful book, *Words by Heart* follows Lena's father's own philosophy: "Nobody needs to be defended . . . just understood."

A Wrinkle in Time, Madeleine L'Engle, *1962, United States,* SCIENCE FICTION, *211 pages*

Meg's father has been gone for too long. A research scientist, Mr. Murry was studying tesseracts, or a fifth dimension of time travel, when he disappeared. Now it is up to Meg, her eerily gifted little brother Charles Wallace, a new friend named Calvin, and three supernatural beings—Mrs. Who, Mrs. Which, and Mrs. Whatsit—to cross the universe and battle evil itself to bring him back. In the process, brilliant, awkward Meg learns much about bravery and her own particular talents. Suspenseful and intriguing, *A Wrinkle in Time* is a well-loved science-fiction classic and the first in a series that readers may want to read in its entirety.

Year of Impossible Goodbyes, Sook Nyul Choi, *1991, Korea,* HISTORI-CAL FICTION, *169 pages*

Year of Impossible Goodbyes is set in Korea during the closing days of World War II and the year that follows. Sook Nyul Choi explores the life-altering ramifications of living in an occupied country through ten-year-old Sookan's experiences and fears. Sookan is surrounded by contradictions. Her mother's Christian beliefs are different from her grandfather's Buddhist faith. She knows she is Korean, yet because the Japanese now occupy her homeland, she is not allowed to speak her language. She longs for her father, who is involved with the resistance movement in Manchuria, and worries about her older brothers, forced to live in Japanese labor camps. As rumors of the Japanese defeat spread through town, Sookan finds reason for hope. Then the slow realization that her country is being divided, and her feelings that the Koreans are trading one form of oppression for another, hurt her to the heart. Sookan's eventual and dangerous escape to the south is so vividly described that readers may feel they are a part of it. Sook Nyul Choi's affecting historical novel, based on her own experiences, is a compelling and heartfelt tribute to a people and place.

Yolanda's Genius, Carol Fenner, *1995, United States,* FICTION, *208 pages*

Yolanda is a big, strong fifth-grader, used to protecting herself and her brother in their tough Chicago neighborhood. When Yolanda's mother moves them to a smaller, safer town, Yolanda is at a bit of a loss. To add to her problems, it is getting harder to know what to do with her little brother, who is as small and thin as Yolanda is large and powerful, and who seems to communicate better through music than through words. Yolanda is sure he is a genius, and readers, who are given insight into his dreamy, sound-obsessed vision of the world, will understand why. But how can Yolanda convince her mother and his teachers, who think he is slow? Yolanda has to figure out who she is and what she wants before she can help anybody else. With her big-boned, life-loving aunt as a model and the unconditional love of her brother to support her, Yolanda discovers what makes her happy.

I've always been good for reading.
                              Christine Hoffman, centenarian

INDEX OF TITLES

Picture Books (1–18)

Storybooks (19–76)

Chapterbooks (77–124)

Moving On (125–190)

INDEX OF AUTHORS

Picture Books (1–18)

Storybooks (19–76)

Chapterbooks (77–124)

Moving On (125–190)

Picture Books (1–18)

Storybooks (19–76)

Chapterbooks (77–124)

Moving On (125–190)

Picture Books (1–18)

Storybooks (19–76)

Chapterbooks (77–124)

Moving On (125–190)

INDEX OF BOOKS BY DATE

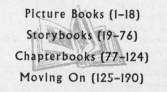

Picture Books (1–18)

Storybooks (19–76)

Chapterbooks (77–124)

Moving On (125–190)

Picture Books (1–18)

Storybooks (19–76)

Chapterbooks (77–124)

Moving On (125–190)

INDEX OF BOOKS BY GENRE

Biographical Fiction

Fantasy / Science Fiction

> **Picture Books (1–18)**
>
> **Storybooks (19–76)**
>
> **Chapterbooks (77–124)**
>
> **Moving On (125–190)**

Fiction

Picture Books (1–18)

Storybooks (19–76)

Chapterbooks (77–124)

Moving On (125–190)

Historical Fiction

Myth / Legend / Folklore

Nonfiction

Poetry

INDEX OF BOOKS BY REGION AND COUNTRY OUTSIDE THE UNITED STATES

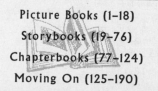

Picture Books (1–18)
Storybooks (19–76)
Chapterbooks (77–124)
Moving On (125–190)

INDEX OF BOOKS BY SUBJECT

Picture Books (1–18)

Storybooks (19–76)

Chapterbooks (77–124)

Moving On (125–190)

African-American Protagonists

Animals

Art

Asian-American Protagonists

Athletics

Aviation and Flight

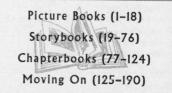

Picture Books (1–18)
Storybooks (19–76)
Chapterbooks (77–124)
Moving On (125–190)

Picture Books (1–18)

Storybooks (19–76)

Chapterbooks (77–124)

Moving On (125–190)

Picture Books (1–18)

Storybooks (19–76)

Chapterbooks (77–124)

Moving On (125–190)

Immigration

Latina Protagonists

Magic

Picture Books (1–18)

Storybooks (19–76)

Chapterbooks (77–124)

Moving On (125–190)

Picture Books (1–18)

Storybooks (19–76)

Chapterbooks (77–124)

Moving On (125–190)

Picture Books (1–18)

Storybooks (19–76)

Chapterbooks (77–124)

Moving On (125–190)